Chapter One

Feather Woods almost jogged to the house. She hadn't been pleased with the way they had gone their separate ways a couple of days ago, and the absence of one of the few friends she had disturbed her greatly. Even though she knew Paige was wrong, she didn't feel the point was worth the argument or the resulting silence between them. Feather would swallow her own pride to apologize for the disagreement, even if she didn't start it. It didn't matter to Feather who was right or not, Paige's friendship was far more important.

Feather took the eight steps, two at a time, up to the front porch. She knocked on the door. When there was no answer, she knocked again. *Paige couldn't still be that upset, could she?* Feather thought as she looked around. Paige's car was in the driveway. Did she catch her friend in the bathroom? She waited a few more minutes before she knocked again. Something wasn't right. She could feel it. She looked around once again. Nothing appeared out of the ordinary.

She looked at the doorknob wondering how she could explain to Paige she found it broken. Peering around again, she figured she would come to that road when needed, but if her sense of dread were factual, she wouldn't need to worry about a broken doorknob. She tried to breathe in anything unusual, but living in a city made odors indistinct. Next door, there was the smell of burnt eggs and bacon that was overwhelmingly pungent.

With a deep, nervous breath, she used her shifter strength to push down hard on the knob until she heard it crack under the intense force. Putting her shoulder to the door, she flung herself against it with enough pressure to push through the entryway only to come to a complete stop as a scream emerged from deep within her very core. The scent of blood hit her only milliseconds before the appalling scene splayed out before her in a disturbing array strewn about the floor.

Feather had seen some horrible sights over the years, but nothing like what was so grotesquely and blatantly displayed before her. She was going to be physically ill from the visage of visceral gore strewn about the foyer. She wasn't absolutely sure she wanted to believe what she was a forced witness to, but the splaying of the limbs and the charred remains of a gold-toned watch still adhered to what was left of her wrist, as well as the intense odor of burnt flesh, could not be denied.

She wanted to turn away, but morbid curiosity intermingled with disbelief had her eyes roaming the remains of her friend, trying to ascertain identifiers because her mind needed constant reaffirmation that the scorched remnants were, in fact, Paige, despite the extreme desire to have the overwhelming evidence point to something contrary. However, in doing so, she was relegated to visions of hollowed-out eye sockets and protruding, blackened sinew and bones from the chest cavity where Paige's heart once resided. What remained of Paige's left breast dangled awkwardly against the floor in a way it never should've been.

That was it. Feather could take no more. She

bolted for the porch where physical evidence of her horror and disgust regurgitated to make itself prominently displayed at her feet. She continued to heave several moments after her stomach expelled the mornings intake of substance, her body refusing to trust it was entirely empty of any and all its contents. Peering down at the mess she made, she was disgusted at herself before she realized it was minor compared to what was behind her in the home.

With shaky hands, she pulled out her phone and dialed 911. Only when she disconnected the call did the immensity of Paige's demise hit her head on. Her friend was gone. Feather had come over to apologize and win her friend back after their argument, and the realization that the last things they said to each other were words of anger crippled Feather emotionally, mentally and physically. Feather's knees gave way and she sunk to the ground in front of the visual evidence of her revulsion over the condition of Paige's remains, a vision she would never forget in a million centuries.

The sirens pierced the otherwise tranquil surroundings, but Feather didn't move as she was too lost in her own grief and regrets. Several padded, heavy steps moved to her and past as they entered the home. Two quickly came back out to make a couple more requests and get the necessary people in to record all evidence of the crime. Another pair of black shoes appeared by Feather and stopped. The man squatted down beside her, helping her stand and move away from the porch to sit in the back seat of a tan sedan with the door kept open and Feather's feet resting on the grassy ground. Again, he squatted beside her trying to get in her line of sight to aid her focus for his line of inquiry.

"Hello. I'm Detective Shaw. Are you the woman who called this in?"

Feather nodded. Shaw noticed how pale her complexion was, how her hands shook, and he was made aware the beautiful woman was in shock over the morbid discovery. He had many questions he would soon need to ask, but he wasn't a total dick, either. He decided to give her a moment so she could catch her breath before he started his inquiries and receive any useful information, or for that matter, an information at all.

"What's your name?" Simple questions would elicit easy answers and get her to focus on the more serious ones he would have to ask in a few minutes.

"Feather. Feather Woods."

Renegade Shaw's head snapped up. He hadn't immediately realized who she was and that surprised him. He gazed over at the other two officers who were some of the first inside, and certainly the first two back out. After calling dispatch for the crime and forensic techs, they had not gone back in. Both were seasoned officers, and for them to not go back inside indicated volumes about the gruesomeness of the crime. He had only adventured into the domicile for a few moments in order to see the extent of the damage, but he realized he had the opportunity to question the witness personally and that took precedence. Getting those first impressions, even skewed by shock, could potentially reveal more than if the subject were fully cohesive, making them more cautious in their responses. Besides, his partner was getting the lay of the land as they waited for the rest of the forensics team to arrive and begin their documentation of the crime scene.

After a few moments he turned back to give his full attention to Feather.

"Do you live here?"

Feather shook her head no.

"Do you know the decedent?"

Feather nodded, tears tumbling down her cheeks in rapid succession. Shaw reached around her to a box of tissues by the back window, offering her some. Feather reached for them absent-mindedly, wiping her cheeks then blowing her nose.

"Can you tell me her name?" Shaw asked.

"Paige. Paige Redmond."

Shaw knew if he could keep her talking she would have something else to focus on, instead of the grisly scene inside.

"How long have you known Paige?"

"Five years. She's my best friend."

"And when did you see her last?"

"A couple of days ago. We had an argument and I came over to apologize. That's when I found her." Again, Feather started to silently weep.

Shaw waited a few more moments letting her mourn her friend before he started the next set of questions. He used the time to size her up. She was very pretty, beautiful even. Long, shiny, ebony hair pulled back, meticulously braided to hang evenly between her shoulder blades. Her eyes were almond shaped, framed by long, lush lashes and deep-amber irises. He had never seen eyes that color before, except when he first met her ages ago. They were amber with gold flecks. Shaw had to physically force himself to look away, they were so enticing. Her skin was a light brown and blended with her eyes perfectly. She was tall and lean with a sinewy but muscular grace. She displayed some characteristics that declared her heritage as Comanche. The slight musky scent she emitted, enhanced by her recent run and the shockingly frightful discovery, declared she was a lioness, an apex predator. He wondered momentarily if she was the guilty culprit, but her anguish and her shock made it extremely doubtful.

He stood. "I'll be right back." Ren moved over to the couple of officers who were outside while keeping his eyes on Feather.

"That's one of the worst things I've ever seen," Officer Harper spoke softly. He was relatively new on the force. A young man just at the start of his career. Although San Antonio experienced a number of deaths and gang violence, they normally weren't this vicious or sadistic.

"I've witnessed quite a lot, but I have to agree with Harper here. What's inside, what was done to that poor woman, is indescribable." Stone Marker was an officer in his mid-forties who had been on the force for twenty-two years. Marker's words of it being one of the most violent deaths he had seen spoke volumes.

As the three of them talked, Ren's partner, Detective Apple Shade, came and joined the group.

Apple, who by the way detested her given name, had been Ren's partner for five years now. An athletic woman, she was petite and usually not noticed for her strength and fortitude, much to the chagrin of some of the criminals who thought them too masculine to be brought down by such a little woman. At least until she proved otherwise, which she had no problem doing. With brown hair cut just below her ears and wire-rimmed glasses, many overlooked her physical attributes because of her lack of height and small stature.

"From what forensics can determine so far, the victim was killed about two this morning. She was already dead when the perp lit her up using an accelerant. Entry was definitely forced. The doorknob is torn clean off, the wood splintered. It was planned, as the fuse to the lights were removed. The rest of the house appears undisturbed. We can rule out robbery gone bad. All her jewelry and electronics are still there.

"Prelims think the perp has done this before. His strokes were sure, no hesitation marks. M.E. is unsure of the weapons at the moment, but there was no visible sign of a struggle. Which, considering the door, is kind of amazing in and of itself.

"The eyes and heart were torn from the body. The eyes post-mortem, the heart when she was still alive. Blood splatter patterns conclude this is the murder scene." Apple looked towards Feather still huddled slightly in a fetal ball. "What's up with the witness?"

"She's pretty shaken up. I'm giving her a minute to let her calm down some before I talk to her some more."

"That's unlike you, Shaw. You going soft on her? Should we take her to H.Q.?"

Shaw's ears turned red at what they hit upon. He had always been, as Apple said, soft on Feather. Even after all the years that had passed, his feelings hadn't abated one iota. He realized that the moment he realized who she was. He wasn't about to admit it, though. Not to Apple or to anyone else, especially when she was majorly involved in such a horrific crime.

"No. I'll get her personal info for when we need to talk to her again. Speaking of which, let me get back to finish my interrogation." As he walked away, Ren knew he was going to have one hell of a job on his hands with this investigation.

As he returned to Feather, he tried to remain sympathetic to her when he took her statement. It was one thing to find your friend deceased, but entirely different to discover such an atrocity committed to a living being.

"Are you ready to answer more questions?"

Feather was never going to be ready, but she nodded yes anyways. She lifted her eyes to him, the first time she had done so since he started talking to her. She was impressed with his good looks. He had broad shoulders, with nice biceps, in a shirt almost too tight to contain his muscular form. His hips were narrow, creating that perfect inverted V that men had. His eyes were a deep, rich chocolate. His nose was slightly hooked, bringing one's attention to his lips, which almost seemed to beg for kisses. His skin was a bit lighter than her own, with a slightly reddish hue. He was a very handsome man, and for some reason she seemed to feel as if she met him once before but couldn't place it. However, a part of her still felt as if she were caught in a surreal nightmare and the déjà vu feeling might just be a result of it. There was a part of her that just wished she could go home and crawl back under the covers to hide from the world, or better yet, wake up and find Paige alive and well. How she wished she could call Paige and vent over the situation, but that was no longer an option. Again, the intensity of her loss and realization that never again would she be able to discuss anything with Paige slammed into her, stealing the very oxygen from her body. Her friend was no longer available to turn to for comfort, or venting, or just a general discussion. It was an incredibly huge gaping hole that made Feather's head literally swim.

Feather had a brother whom she was extremely close to, but her older sibling didn't quite get some of her ideas or beliefs, especially if they were women related. Only Paige conversed with her about those things. Feather realized she needed her brother, Raine. She needed his strength, his guidance and his comfort as she told him about what happened.

While Shaw had been talking to the other officers, giving her a few moments to gather her thoughts together, Feather sent a mental connection to Raine. Not all shifters could telepathically communicate, but siblings, especially those who were emotionally close, faired a better chance to do so.

Usually, Feather hated talking that way to him, but she was so discombobulated and desperate she didn't give sending him a mental communiqué a second thought. Closing her eyes, she focused on sending out the mental call. *Raine? Raine! I need you.*

Raine's head snapped up. He knew something must be terribly wrong for her to contact him telepathically. He was well aware of how much she detested that type of communication. No matter how old they were, he would always be there for her. He had accepted responsibility for taking care of her ever since they were children.

He linked her back immediately, concern clearly palatable in the response. *Where are you? What happened?*

I'm in front of Paige's, she managed to respond. Her mind was all over the place and it was an effort to concentrate in order to talk to him as it was.

Paige's? he growled back. *Don't tell me. You gave in and she refused your apology. Now you're upset and want me to get you.*

Feather shook her head, even though she knew Raine couldn't see her. *She's dead. She was murdered.*

Raine's demeanor instantly changed. *How?* Although Paige was human with a finite life expectancy, she was young and shouldn't be deceased this early in her human cycle. He knew something was terribly amiss and he instantly wondered if his sister killed the human by accident. That would explain so much.

It's horrible, Raine. Just horrible.

I'll be there in a few minutes. I'm on my way, sis.

* * *

Shaw pulled out his notes once again before he started his questions back up. He hoped he had given her enough time to get her mind wrapped around the circumstances a bit more. "Does Ms. Redmond have any family we should contact?"

Feather was brought out of her silent contemplation; a sense of relief flooded within her knowing Raine was on his way. He was her anchor ever since they were children, assuming the role of big brother, guardian, protector and sometimes even parent, when need be.

"She has a sister in California. Marley. Her sister is married. I don't remember the last name. Sorry."

"That's fine. We'll figure it out. No parents?"

"No. They are both deceased."

"Where did she work?"

"She is a hostess for Le Chic Restaurant. I mean, was."

"Do you know of anyone who might want her dead?"

Feather peered up at Shaw like he just told her the sky was green and the grass was pink.

"No. She's too sweet and friendly."

"What about a boyfriend or an ex?"

Feather shook her head again. "Her last boyfriend was Greg, but they broke up about seven months ago. He was transferred by his employment and it was a mutual decision to split."

"Where did he move to?"

"Milwaukee, Wisconsin."

"She hasn't been seeing anyone else since?"

"No. It was what we had fought about. She wanted to go to some bars to do this speed dating thing on Saturday. I don't feel those men are in it for a serious relationship. She called me a stick in the mud and tried to force me to sign up. When I refused, well, you know."

Shaw nodded, making notes as they conversed. "What about at work? Anyone there she might not have gotten along with? Anyone who might have been jealous of her?"

"No. Not that I'm aware of. She was a kind person. Helpful. Sweet. She volunteers for several organizations, helping however she is able."

"Which ones? Which organizations?"

"The Humane Society, and the homeless shelters and food kitchens."

A commotion caught Shaw's attention and he stood to make sure he and his witness were safe from whatever was going on nearby. A man was trying to push past the perimeter officers, forcefully making his way to them.

Feather also heard the disturbance and got out of the back of the car she had been sitting in, sensing her brother. She ran to him and he quickly gathered her up in his arms. The officers who were protesting as they followed him, trying to get him to halt his progress, stopped themselves when they saw Shaw. Shaw waved them off as he moved closer to the couple. Seeing they were not needed, they went back to their perimeter posts.

Shaw walked up to the couple. He should've guessed someone so beautiful wouldn't be available, even if her friend wanted to go to meet men. No wonder they got into a fight. Feather was probably as loyal as they came. The man with her now was tall and lean with well-muscled arms and a tawny complexion. He was large and enveloped Feather with his arms to the point she was almost lost against him, swallowed up by his body against hers.

When he reached the couple, the male moved her alongside of him, then slightly behind himself in a very protective movement. His hazel eyes seemed to glare at him, but Shaw was not about to be intimated.

Shaw stopped in front of him. "And you are?"

"Raine."

"Detective Shaw. Did you know Paige Redmond?"

"Yes. Only because she was Feather's friend.

She wasn't my friend or anything. Just an acquaintance." Raine still wasn't quite sure what had occurred, but knew his instincts of something more drastic occurring was correct. He only hoped with fervor Feather didn't kill the woman. She was in the back of the police car when he arrived and surely that couldn't be any good. "Are you done questioning her?" Raine asked, anxious to get Feather away from the police and find out what kind of quality control he was going to have to implement.

"For the moment. I'll be in contact again later."

Raine nodded, pulling his sister along to get her away quickly and safely before the detective changed his mind and arrested her. Raine led her to his Ninja motorcycle. He got on and started the engine while she climbed on behind him, wrapping her arms around his waist in order to not fall off.

Shaw stood watching the two of them leave. Only when they were no longer within his sight did he turn and steel himself for the scene inside the house.

Chapter Two

1892

Feather stood on the edge of the hill, the wind billowing her hair behind her. Her people were unique in a way. Although some remained by Fort Sill, many others headed south towards Texas after their boarding school years. Most didn't have modern skills. They were trained instead for blacksmithing and farming, even though the industrial age was beginning to excel.

Feather should've been a domestic—either a maid or a cook or both—but again, she and her people were special.

She heard the animal behind her and turned to watch the tawny-furred mountain lion stealthily approach.

"You can't sneak up on me, brother," she teased him lightly. She held her hand out and Raine moved into her palm, pushing his head against it, using his nose over and over to rub her hand in affection.

Are you sure you want to do this? He sent the thought into her head, the only way he could speak to her when in his current form. Sure, he could've shifted back into human form and talked to her like a man, but he liked being the lion of the America's, enjoyed the apex alpha he was in his animal-spirit form.

There were many Native Americans that had been blessed by the Great Spirit, the Great Manitou, or whatever the particular tribe called their Supreme Being. As with all Native Americans, they had a spirit to guide them in their life's journeys, to aid them in the path they should take, but the Great Spirit decreed one group from each tribe would be able to shift into the animal that guided each particular person. They alone would not only embody the wisdom and soul of their guide, but also embody each of their special attributing aspects. They would have the magic bestowed upon them to alter their human states into the creature that would lead them throughout their lives, as well as be gifted with additional powers, which varied per the individual. These powers were as varied as the animals that guided them.

Feather was quiet for a moment. She had blossomed into a very beautiful young woman, curvy in all the right places. Raine hated she was so beautiful and caught the eye of many males over the past couple of years. As her big brother, he'd always taken it upon himself to watch over and care for her. He knew the time would come when she would no longer need his guidance and protection. He just despaired that the day was looming upon him faster than he desired.

She knew her decision was a difficult one and affected not only herself, but her brother and the village as well. She was gifted. Although Raine figured she would always be special because he loved her, her gifts soon started to develop in a different way, which would lead her down an unexpected path. When her powers began to emerge in the boarding school and her beauty gained attention there as well, Raine knew what he had to do. He grabbed Feather and they ran back to their tribe. Once there, he avoided his father and appealed to the Elders' Council to aid in hiding them.

Feather's powers had grown exponentially in just a few months of hiding. Extremely rare for a woman, the council realized she needed to be trained appropriately and her education couldn't be near the rest of the village. Raine had always taken care of her, was always by her side, but this was something she had to do alone. It would be the first time they would be separated and Raine was far from being happy about it.

"Yes. I'm sure. You know as well as I, I need to do this. Besides, it's a great honor to have been chosen."

When do you leave?

"Tomorrow. I'll take the train that leaves at ten a.m. I'm kind of excited. I've never been on an Iron Horse before." Feather turned to look at him, her hand still rubbing that spot between his ears. "I know you're not pleased with my leaving. Will you be alright while I'm away?"

I'll manage without you, somehow.

"No, you won't." Feather smiled. "You're going to be lost without me to mother hen over."

Are you kidding me? I'm going to throw a party to celebrate not having to watch over you every moment of every day, he teased back, his laughter filling her head as hers filled the air about them. Raine's teasing helped to lessen the tension in the air.

Feather stopped rubbing his ears and turned back to the view in front of them. "A part of me is scared," she said simply.

He shook his massive head and nudged her hand. *You don't have to do this, just because the Elders said.*

She turned back to him, crouching down to put her arms around his coarse-furred neck. "I know. Just as you know I can't go against them. I'm scared because it's new and different, and for the first time in our lives we will be apart. I'll be out there and you'll be here with father."

I'm bigger and stronger. He can't hurt me. The training will help you and it's something we can't do for you here.

"I understand. Still, I wish you could be nearby. Away from him and close to me. What if I need you?"

Then you link me and I'll be there as quick as I can. Feather, I'll always be here whenever you may need me. Only our locations will change. Nothing else will. You're my baby sister. I love you and I'll always protect and care for you, even if—no, when—you're more powerful than me.

"And I'll always need you, brother," she replied softly.

* * *

Present

Back at the station, Detective Renegade Shaw sat at his desk. He had made sure all the information was in the correct hands to be investigated properly;

the criminologists, forensics, morgue, and labs were all involved in testing every fiber, micro-organism, angle of injury, whatever it took to put together the timeline of events as well as the clues it would take to find the culprit who did such a dastardly deed. Now he had to wait until the tests were completed and they got back to him with the results and, hopefully, information he could use.

In the meantime, he had a good number of notes to type up, as well as the order of interviews he wanted to still conduct. He opened the first page of his notes with Feather. He still couldn't believe it. After all these years. She didn't remember him. That was obvious and a great disappointment. He had to admit, it took him a few moments to realize it was her. The scent and then her eyes gave her away. Those eyes were too unique to not recognize her. She, however, didn't seem to know him. Even if she were in complete shock, he thought he would have at least registered within her memory. Albeit, he only talked to her once many decades ago, but thinking he hadn't been that memorable disturbed him somewhat.

He had been young and scrawny back then. A child pretending to be a man, sent into the world with outdated skills and needing to figure out his own path in this world. She was as beautiful as he remembered, but even more mature and wise from the child he'd met briefly a couple of hundred years ago.

1892

Ren was nearing the end of his specialized training when she first arrived. He had been sent to get the new students from the train station and welcome them to the camp. There were only five: Feather, Silver, Payne, Uxem and Austin. He knew beforehand that Feather would be the youngest out of the group. He also assumed they would be together when they got off the train. Not many alighted at this particular station, so he doubted he would have to worry which ones they were.

Feather was the smallest of the five standing on

the platform, unsure of where to go or what to do next. She stood out to Ren immediately. Something about her called to him and he was immediately smitten over her. He couldn't appear too zealous in wanting to assist her and be by her side. He didn't want to make the others feel less, so he pushed his sudden, ardent feelings down and tried to act normal.

"Grab your belongings and follow me. I'm assuming you can all ride?"

The three men nodded without hesitation, as did Silver, but Feather was too busy looking around at the wonders of the area to respond, until he approached her directly to gain her attention. "Can you ride? If not, you can ride with me." *Please, don't be able to ride*, he pleaded silently to himself.

Feather peered up at him wide-eyed. "Sorry. Yes. I'm Nemene."

That was answer enough. Comanche were taught to ride before they could barely walk. By the ages of 5 or 6, boys were given a bow and arrow to hunt and be a warrior, taught by their grandfather.

Women taught the girls how to gather food and cook, but they all knew how to ride. It also said something about Feather's emerging powers. At age 14, Comanche girls were usually ready for marriage. If Feather was here for training, her budding powers must be fairly impressive.

Ren led them to where six horses were tied up and waiting. He took the Paint and let the others choose their own. Sitting astride, he waited while they moved to a horse, secured their belongings and mounted. Ren watched them all, but his focus continuously returned to the youngest in the group. His fascination with her didn't waver one iota.

When all were ready, Ren led them away from the station towards the foothills of the Guadalupe Mountains. Part of his duties were to make sure all the newcomers were situated, and then he was to report to the head medicine man, Xulth, that the students were settled in.

Once they arrived, he told the group which tipi's they were to use and took the horses from them to put in the corral where others would make sure they were brushed, fed and cared for. Ren proceeded to quickly check on the new students, not that it was needed or even a part of his duties, but he figured he could see her again and be inconspicuous if he checked on all of them. Of course, he saved Feather's tipi for last.

"Just checking to make sure you're doing alright." Ren shifted nervously from foot to foot. She sent all sorts of butterflies into his stomach and groin he'd never felt before. In the past, he had been too busy dealing with his powers and training than to worry about finding a woman of his own. However, Feather just twisted his insides into every which way. He had to admit those feelings were alien to him and it didn't help his condition when she stood before him looking so small and frightened. It gave her a helpless look. He wanted to step in and take charge to remove it. He wanted to pull her to him, hold her close, protect her from the world, and claim her for his very own. He wondered what she would feel like in his arms, what she would taste like with her lips against his and, most of all, he wondered what she would look like with a smile touching her face. Would her eyes glow with happiness along with her smile?

Though a smile seemed the furthest thing from her mind at the moment; she looked so lost and unsure. He took a step closer, trying not to intimidate her in any way. He repeated the question, every word laced with concern. He stepped even further into her tipi. She was alone inside. Walking up to her, he gently placed his forefinger under her chin to tilt her head up and that's when the depth of her amber eyes hit him like a slap in the face. It was a color he'd never seen and it gave her such a unique quality. He was more smitten with her than he was just five minutes before.

"Tell me what has you so upset?"

Feather looked up into his deep chocolate eyes. Something inside told her she could trust this young man even though she didn't know him. "It's the first time I've been away from home by myself. I'm not sure what's going to happen here."

She's a bit homesick, Ren thought. Not unusual

for the young who came here. He understood, sympathized and tried to alleviate her concerns to make her more comfortable. Ren pulled her into a tight hug, holding her close. He couldn't help but breathe in her scent in the process, shutting his eyes as he memorized it. "It'll be okay. Tomorrow and in the days forward you'll be so busy, you won't have time to miss your family. And before you know it, you will be back home with your village."

"I've never been totally alone before. I know I shouldn't ask this, but would you stay with me? Just for tonight?"

Ren knew she didn't know what she was asking of him, but he also knew he couldn't deny her either. "I'll stay, but I have to inform Xulth that all of you are here and settled for the night. I'll be back in fifteen minutes and if you still want me to remain with you, I will. In the meantime, why don't you unpack your bed roll and stoke up the fire."

"Thank you," she said quietly and moved to the belongings she had brought with her.

She had just finished up when Ren returned,

carrying his own blanket draped over his arm. "Do you still desire me to keep you company?" A part of him so hoped she did, and another wondered how he was going to be so close to her and not touch her. If they were anywhere else but at the training camp, he wouldn't even be allowed to get this near alone without a chaperon or a bonding on the table. Otherwise he would be taking her all night long and claiming her in the morning to the rest of the world. Some might use her and throw her away, but he was not that kind of a man. He would be respectful, no matter how hard it was going to be.

"Yes, please." She was so innocent, she had no knowledge that asking him to stay was not the appropriate thing to request. All she thought about was not being alone. All her life she has had someone with her; whether it was her brother or the other girls at the boarding school with her brother just down the hall, she was never totally alone. Until now, that is, and the idea made her timid.

Ren pulled out his blanket and moved to the other side of the tipi. There was no way in hell he could be any closer and respect her enough to not touch her. Besides, he didn't want to cause her any problems by staying in her space. If he were smart about it, he would've sent Silver here. It would have been more appropriate, but he was selfish and wanted even these few hours with her alone. What got into him he was truly unaware, but he also wasn't going to fight against it. Not entirely. He would revere her honor and not disrespect her in any way, no matter how much he wanted to touch her. They spent the night with the fire between them, talking. Their discussions consisted of boarding schools the Natives were being forced into, the attempted genocide of Native American culture by the Anglo-Saxons, the takeover of their lands by Europeans who seemed to have little or no respect for it, and a bit about the training she was about to partake in.

Before he knew it, the sun was starting to rise and he quietly left her tipi so as not to alert others to his presence there all night.

Present

Until just a few hours ago, that was the last time Renegade Shaw had seen her. He thought her lost to him forever. Always searching, never finding what happened to her. Suddenly, she was in his life as quickly as he had left hers all those years before.

Det. Shaw looked down at the notepad he had been fingering for the past couple of minutes. Just like then, she took his breath away and made him forget what he should be doing. Rubbing his face, he moved to grab a cup of coffee before returning to his desk and start his report.

Chapter Three

1890

The teen grabbed his younger sister's hand and pulled her out of bed to hide. Not that there was much room to remain undiscovered. His father's voice was loud and boisterous, angry as he talked to whoever met him just outside the entrance to his abode.

The youth blocked his sister from view, trying to protect her as best as a fourteen-year-old is able from a grown drunken man. He prayed to the gods, who he hoped might be listening tonight, that his father would come in and just pass out on his sleeping mat. Raine hoped the white man's firewater would entice Storm to rest instead of give him the desire to beat his children for imagined wrongs to which his father felt was done to him. Or maybe it was because Storm Woods realized he could take out his frustrations with gods and government on his children, who couldn't properly defend themselves. Although the Nemene put their children first, that was when one's faculties weren't diminished by alcohol.

Raine Woods was fully aware Storm was a virtual powder keg when he was full of firewater and the best way to protect himself and his little sister, Feather, was to make sure they were quiet and unseen until Storm passed out. Sadly, Raine didn't think he would be so lucky tonight. He could only hope to keep Feather out of his father's crosshairs, especially since he had already failed his mother, Suni.

The vision of Storm hitting Suni so hard six years ago, pushing her into the fire pit, would last with him for a lifetime. (For a shifter like him, that could be a very long time, if he survived his father's abuse.) As his mother tripped back from the force of the blow and into the flame, Suni's dress caught fire, which quickly engulfed her body. Her screams of agony echoed as she flailed outside the structure. Raine should've gone out to help his mother, should've helped protect her from Storm's wrath. Raine should've done something instead of cower against the corner, blocking a very frightened Feather from the horror he was witness to. He pulled Feather against his boyish chest, almost smothering her to prevent her from ever observing such a horrific sight.

Storm followed Suni out, shutting off the view of their injured mother, but the scent of burning flesh continued to overwhelm the interior. Raine did his best to comfort his sister, but he should've left Feather and gone outside to assist his mother. If he admitted it to himself, though, he knew protecting Feather was not the entire reason for staying with her. Nor was his own youthfulness. He was already considered a good hunter, taught as all young men were by their grandfathers. However, he was scared and dealing with several bruises on his youthful body. The idea of provoking his father further terrified him. He knew as a hunter he shouldn't allow himself to be so frightened, but though there was an adoration for children in the tribe, there was also a strong sense of respecting one's elders. He was definitely in a quandary and chose the safest route.

Six years later, Raine was still riddled with guilt. He could've gone out there and at least tried to do something. Would crossing over have been any worse than his day to day terror? Without his mother to protect them, Raine and Feather took on increased punishments. His mother survived her burns for a couple of years, but she never fully recovered. Storm was contrite, laying off the firewater for the first few months she still lived, then increased his drinking, but not as heavily, at least not until she finally passed away. Only then did he return to imbibing even more heavily than before.

Raine wasn't sure Feather could handle another beating by Storm. He failed his mother; he would not fail his baby sister. She was his to protect as best as he was possibly able.

"Please, let him be too tired and just fall asleep. Please." Raine prayed almost silently to whomever or whatever might hear him to grant his wish.

Yet, it wasn't to be as Storm bounded through the door and immediately looked around for his two offspring. Storm was not a good or nice drunk as it was, but he was particularly furious at the moment. He was a violent man to begin with and alcohol only made him meaner. He hated life. He detested his spawn and the fact he had to care for them. They took what little he made to clothe and feed when he would much rather trade it in for alcohol. He wouldn't have married or had children if he hadn't been forced into it.

When the cholera plague ravaged their village in 1870, the men of the tribe were forced to take brides to repopulate, whether or not they wanted them. Storm didn't want a wife but he had no choice. So, he chose Suni. At least she was young, quiet and undemanding. She did what she was required to do and never spoke poorly of her decisions. When she birthed Raine and, two years later, Feather, she took care of them, leaving Storm to his own pursuits.

A very small part of Storm regretted Suni dying. She was a loyal and faithful woman, but more important to him, she took care of the young. Now he was stuck with the responsibility and he wasn't too thrilled. Less tonight than usual.

Storm had been informed Raine had been setting fires in the field. Had he known anything about anything, he might have realized the beginning obsession started with Suni's demise. Storm didn't care nor would he, even if he had known. What he was aware of was that he was now responsible for the actions of his son, which only served to infuriate him further.

Storm stopped just inside the entryway, letting his eyes adjust to the dim interior. When he saw Raine and Feather in the corner, he stomped their way, a murderous, drunken glaze in his eyes.

Raine had nowhere to go. He could only stand, blocking Feather from Storm's reach, but Storm had no interest in his weeping, sniveling, cowering daughter. Instead, he reached out with a slightly unsteady hand, gripped Raine's shirt by the collar and literally tossed the fourteen-year-old youth to the other end of the floor.

Feather didn't move, instead curling up into as small of a ball as she could, burying her face against her knees. Storm didn't give her a second thought. His sole focus was on his son.

"So, I hear you like to play with fire!" Storm's words slurred a bit, but they could still be made out.

As Raine stumbled near the door, he fell to his knees. He knew this was going to be bad, worse even than any time before. He might even be killed, just as his mother had been. Sure, Suni lasted for four years after being burned, but she was never well and never the same. The burns and her lack of will to live sealed her fate, it just took longer for her body to catch up.

Raine should run, but he also knew if he did, he would be leaving Feather alone. He couldn't do that. As much as he hated having to take the role of being Feather's parent since he was eight, he promised his mother to protect her. He agreed to the responsibility. He failed his mother once, he wouldn't do it again. Not unless he had no choice, such as if he were dead. A vision of his mother on fire once again entered his mind. He would never get the smell of her burning flesh out of his memory. The smell of his mother cooking like some roasted deer over a pit, but sweeter and more poignant as well, wasn't like anything he'd ever perceived before or since.

"No. I don't," Raine replied.

"Arrow saw you! Said you set the bush fire by his place. The one that burned his home down. Do you really think you can do anything around here without someone being a witness? Now I have to pay for his losses with money I don't have or goods I can't supply because I used the goods I traded for food for you and your sister!"

Raine almost snorted at the absurdity of his father's statement. "No, you didn't!" he snapped back. He was probably going to walk in the shadows of death soon, so why should he remain quiet? "You spent it on booze, just like always. I trade or hunt for what Feather and I need! We subsist on tripe, rats, lizards, skunks and frogs when the hunting is sparse. Since I can't leave Feather long, I can't afford to go on the big hunting trips. I'm doing your job as a parent.

"As for the fire, it was an accident. I'll help him rebuild, as I told him I would. He should never have brought you into it when I promised to make reparations." Raine usually gave most of his share to Feather, making sure she got enough food to help her grow appropriately. He was the older brother. He would make sure she was cared for, even if it meant starving himself.

Storm hit him and broke his reverie; the angry throb spread across his cheek in pulsating intense anguish. Raine was still trying to comprehend the first hit when Storm pulled on his arm, slugging the youth across his face again.

Raine refused to cry out, despite all he was put through, and it infuriated Storm even more. Storm didn't stop. He wanted to hear his son beg for mercy. In his intoxicated state, Storm wanted the boy to hurt as much as he did for his unhappy life.

In the process, he didn't care who else was unhappy. Storm doubted he would grant any beneficence, but he still wanted to hear Raine ask Storm to show him mercy.

Feather couldn't stand the sounds of hitting and the grunts of force. Uncurling from her position, she ran to her father and pulled on his buckskin shirt, pleading for him to stop.

"Don't hurt him anymore. Stop! Please, stop!"

Storm backhanded her as his response. She crumpled near the center pole, sobbing.

Storm returned his attention to Raine when a pounding came from outside. Growling, Storm looked up in mid-swing. He never had visitors and it startled him to temporary immobility. The second knock came, more insistent than the first. Considering the knock came on a buffalo-hide-covered structure, the fact it resounded at all was amazing. Storm lifted the flap and stepped outside. As he disappeared from the interior, Feather ran over to Raine and the two huddled in the back behind the fire pit, the light from the flames dancing ominous shadows across their youthful, worried faces.

Several agonizing minutes passed before Storm returned. Raine immediately became more concerned. He'd seen many moods of his father, but relaxed or happy was not among them. Yet Storm appeared calmer than Raine ever remembered him being.

"Grab your sleeping rolls, both of you, and your extra clothes. Actually, get all of your belongings together."

Raine followed the directives for both, unsure what was going to happen. Since they had very little, it didn't take Raine long to get everything together. When they were ready, Storm led the children outside. Some members of the village were standing there, the Tribal Peace Chief in the forefront. Behind them, several U.S. soldiers were waiting. One pointed to a wagon indicating they and their meager belongings would get on it. Raine took Feather's hand, leading her, but looked back several times at Storm. Once Storm felt they were secure enough, he ducked back into the tipi, letting the flap close.

He sadly wondered what he did to get both himself and Feather sent away from the entire village. He'd told Arrow he was sorry and he'd help him rebuild. Did the village hate him for the accident? Were they being punished as a result? He wanted to apologize to the Peace Chief, beg they keep Feather at least, but one look at them told him his words would be futile.

Raine held Feather against him as the wagon pulled away, watching the only home, the only village they'd ever known, slowly fade away.

Chapter Four

Present

Silver Swimming Otter moved silently about her apartment, checking doors and windows to make sure they were properly secured. Rubbing the ears of her mixed Persian cat, she scooped Whiskers up and carried her into the kitchen to get her food while she made herself a sandwich for her own dinner. Peering out the window, it was just starting to rain. Normally, she loved the quiet drops on her window, but today, they seemed to foretell a warning she couldn't quite fathom. She was probably just being silly. Still, the shroud of doom didn't ease in any way.

Putting it out of her mind as best she could, she focused on giving Whiskers her meal before sitting down with her own, pulling out the newspaper she picked up on her way home from work to read as she ate. She jumped when she heard a tapping at her window, then laughed at herself when she realized it was a tree branch banging from the wind.

"I don't know why I'm so nervous tonight, Whiskers." She would often talk to the cat. It was something she felt people who lived alone with animals often did, as they were companions and very good listeners. A few minutes later, there was another clang against the windows, but she ignored it. Moments of silence passed before the sound of glass breaking made her jump so much her chair tipped backwards with her in it.

It took a moment to catch her breath and stand. Grabbing a couple of towels and a broom, she headed to the other room where shards of broken glass were lying on the floor. "Great. I'll have to call the super to repair the window and maybe have him trim the tree as well."

Moving towards the mess, she started to sweep but felt a presence behind her. She spun, sure it was just Whiskers and needing to keep her away so he wouldn't cut her paws accidentally. Only, it wasn't Whiskers.

He looked familiar, and yet she couldn't place him. His rain-soaked clothes were plastered to his rock-hard body, and at some other time she might have wanted to enjoy what his body said it could offer. She barely registered his presence, her mouth opening to scream, when he was beside her with a swiftness not found in humans. His hand covered her mouth to muffle her shrieks. He leaned over, close to her ear. "Shh."

She didn't listen, but instead struggled to get away. She bit his hand and he yelped as he pulled it back swiftly, using it to backhand her. Her head twisted with the force and she remained turned away as she spat out a bit of blood before turning back to face him. She raised her hands to cast a binding spell, but as she faced him, their eyes met and she froze, her arms still up in the air.

"Lower your arms," he commanded, taking a step closer to his hypnotized prey.

She did as he instructed, remaining motionless, waiting. Whiskers hid under the table, her huge green eyes peering unblinkingly at the couple.

Not breaking eye contact, for he needed it to maintain his mesmerizing spell, he removed his soaked clothing from his body, letting it fall to the floor in a wet heap. He was hard, excited. His blood pumped rapidly throughout his body. He had always taken great enjoyment in the hunt and more in the kill. Even the poignant, sweet smell of burning flesh got him titillated. He enjoyed being able to take his time, prolong the experience. Tonight was no exception.

He kept eye contact as he opened his mouth, forcing hers to open with his thumbs. A white adumbration streamed out of her orifice and into his waiting maw. She could feel her organs shrivel in response to the loss of her soul. Once her spirit had been removed from her vessel, he moved closer, keeping his eyes on hers until the very last moment as he neared her neck. His fangs tore into her skin just as his hand plunged into her rib cage to grip her pounding heart. He drank of her blood, feeling her heartbeat slow down as he did so and eventually stop altogether. Her eyes were still wide with shock and surprise, but the life within her had fled. As he pulled his blood-soaked mouth from her neck, he also pulled his hand free from her body, still clutching the heart.

Her body plopped to the floor with a heavy clunk. As he stood over her, he feasted on her once-pumping organ, a slight smile to his lips, his free hand pumping his engorged member. He finished his meal just as he was about to come, ejaculating onto his wet clothes to avoid any DNA accidently being left at the scene.

Bending over, he grabbed the towel she had brought into the room with her to clean up the rain and used it to clean himself, throwing the cloth onto his clothes when he was finished. He knelt over her, reaching with nails like talons, and plucked out one eye, sucking it clean, then the other, putting both in the bag he usually wore around his waist. His trophies of his rescues and his most prized possessions. He could look at them any time and remember which eyes belonged to his victims and what they tasted like as he ate their life's blood and heart.

Chapter Five

Det. Ren Shaw looked over the prelim reports that had come in so far from the forensics and crime investigation teams. From the various statements, the guy he was tracking was a total sicko, but it was obvious he was skilled at what he was doing. Which meant he'd done it before. He put out a search to try and find cases with similar MOs. Exsanguinated, eyes removed, heart removed, body burned, and where the autopsy showed older organs than could be accounted for, or a combination thereof would suffice. It didn't surprise him he found over fifty cases dating back to 1939, but only fifteen seemed relevant to being the same perp. The others were missing key components to the current crimes. The ones that seemed like they were possibly connected dated back to 1948 and were found in the Kansas, Oklahoma, and Texas areas. Ren wondered if they went back even further, but technology wasn't as proficient back then to have made the crimes more noticeable. He would need to look at the pattern and see if he could find a common denominator. Then he got the notice of another, sixteenth, case. Only, this one was fresh, and it was also a name he recognized, but wasn't sure why it was familiar.

Grabbing his jacket, he hurriedly got into his vehicle and sped over to the location of the new crime scene, alerting the officers on scene of his imminent arrival. To have another murder like this within just a couple of days of the last sent warning bells off all over the place. The other fifteen, which fit the previous MOs and were possibly done by the same perp, mostly occurred years apart. So what had set him off that he upped the time table to just a couple of days between killings? Was this going to be the new trend? Would they be able to get him off the streets before he moved on and laid low again, making him even more difficult to apprehend? Before he killed again?

Ren didn't want this to become one of the multitudes of cold cases left unsolved for more decades than he cared to imagine. However, something about this whole thing bothered him. It seemed familiar in an odd way and yet not, but he couldn't quite put his finger on it. Whatever familiarity there was remained, tickling the back part of his memory, and he was aware it would be when he wasn't thinking about it that the answer would come to him. Still, he almost feared the answer and the revelations it might illuminate.

He called his partner, who was tracking down another lead, and asked her to meet him at the new crime scene. She would join him there when she finished her business. Hopefully she would be able to gather more conclusive information about the guy doing all this shit. The sooner they could get him behind bars, the happier Ren would be.

He parked his black 1970 GTO and headed past the yellow police tapes, showing his badge to the officers guarding the perimeter. They let him pass and he headed into the three-flat apartment building. There was no question where the crime scene was as some police lingered about while others were taking down statements from potential witnesses.

As he entered the flat, he stopped. A feeling of

déjà vu hit him hard and he looked around, not sure why as he was fairly positive he'd never been here before. Shaking off his irrational feeling, he proceeded inside and searched for the lead officer on the case. Det. Walter Gattion noticed him immediately and headed his way.

Introducing himself, Ren proceeded to ask if the victim was burnt after having their eyes and heart removed from the body. Walter seemed saddened as he realized Ren had a similar case. Quickly comparing notes, Walter turned the investigation over to Ren, who had seniority on the case since he caught the first one. At least, the first one they were aware of in the area.

Imagine Ren's surprise when one of the other officers from outside came in to state the victim had a very distraught friend named Feather Woods. It was then it clicked for him. Silver was one of the students in the training camp at the same time as Feather. He quickly made a note to check the other decimated victims and see if they had any connection to Feather or her family. It might be the link he had been searching for, which would connect the dots in all the murders. Checking a few other things first, he then headed out to meet with Feather, who was in total shock and almost in a catatonic state. He couldn't blame her. In just a matter of days, two women Feather knew ended up mutilated and dead.

However, Ren also couldn't help wonder if she was behind it. After all, what were the odds she would know both victims? Or that she would appear at both crime scenes shortly after they occurred? He was never one for coincidences, despite the magical things he knew about and could do himself. The question was, did she have a motive? She certainly had opportunity for the first murder. Did she for this one as well? What about the others that he tracked across the country? Where was she when those happened?

Feather looked up, recognition in her eyes as she saw Ren approach her. She felt almost sick to her stomach as he strode towards her. She knew. If she had any doubts before, they evaporated the moment he came out the door and headed her way. Her knees buckled and she fell onto the grass, trying to keep the nausea down to a tolerable not-throw-up-on-his-shiny-shoes level. In her line of sight, those shoes appeared as he squatted down in front of her. Out of nowhere, a bottle of water appeared in her vision and she gratefully, albeit shakily, took it. She dry heaved a few moments, but the water helped to settle her enough to not actually vomit. Soft fur brushed against her hand. Surprised, she jumped slightly and noticed a beautiful Persian cat with green eyes against the leg her hand had been resting on. She reached out to pet it, wondering where it might have come from.

The poor thing looked scared and sad, and suddenly she knew. Her own feline senses let her get glimpses into the cat's mind. Visions of Silver appeared in Feather's head. She rested a hand on Whiskers' back, knowing that was her name. Once she calmed down, she peered up at him.

"Thank you for the water." She paused, setting the bottle on the lawn beside her. "It's Silver. She is…like Paige?" She knew the answer, but she had to really hear it from him to believe.

"Yes," Ren answered. "You knew her." It wasn't a question, but a comment. He realized she still didn't recognize him from her long-distant past and a part of him was disappointed in that fact. She had made such a huge impression on him, and he was barely a spot on her radar. Talk about tearing out one's heart.

"Yeah. For many years."

"I know. Ever since power training at the camp."

Feather's head snapped up to peer at him in astonished surprise. "How?"

"You don't remember me?"

She shook her head and thought back to that time in the camp. She stuck mostly with the females for her training, not giving the men much notice since they were trained separately for the most part. "No. I'm sorry."

"I picked you up from the train when you first arrived." He hoped it would be enough to jar her memory. When the light of recognition appeared in her eyes, he knew it was.

"I'm sorry! I do remember you. I never did get your name, but you spent the night in my tipi keeping me company that first night. I was so timid and scared about being away from home. I'd forgotten. How'd I forget such respectful kindness?"

He shrugged. "It's not important." He knew he was lying. To him it was extremely important. He was still taken with her, and for her to dismiss him so easily saddened him. She didn't need to know his feelings, especially not with everything else currently going on. If it was meant to be, then in time, she would come to him of her own accord. "When is the last time you saw her?"

"It had been years since I'd spoken or seen her, but last week she contacted me. We had an appointment today to meet for tea. She seemed like she had something important to tell me, but she said we would discuss it in person."

"No idea what it was in reference to?"

"No. I admit I was surprised to hear from her. As I said, it had been years since we had been in contact. She just said she had something to tell me and it needed to be discussed in person."

Ren helped her up and moved her to the back of a squad car so she could sit. She grabbed Whiskers before she followed him to the car. He needed a moment to think about what Feather just disclosed. Again, the coincidence greatly bothered him.

"That your cat?"

Feather shook her head. "Not really. It was Silver's. She's scared and seems to have come to me for protection."

Shaw nodded. "It would be most appropriate. Animals can sense our guides, and as a mountain lion, you'd be the logical choice. Can you talk to it? Maybe get a description of the culprit?"

"Although she was there, she didn't move out from under the table. She said he was wet from the rain and he took his clothes off and left them piled on the floor until he left. For once, she wasn't curious enough to check him out. She sensed his volatile attitude." She reached down, her hand soothing the fur on Whiskers' back. "May I keep her? She now needs a new home."

He shrugged. "I don't see why not. It's not like she can testify or anything. I don't think the courts will accept a Dr. Dolittle scenario in court." Of course, he was referring to the 1967 Rex Harrison portrayal and the court scene where he was accused of killing a little old lady who was, in fact, a sea lion he was helping to get free.

He barely got her situated in the vehicle when he heard a motorcycle pull up nearby. Looking, he recognized her boyfriend, Raine, coming to collect her again. His ire rose, but only his clenched jaw was any indication of his irritation. "Stay here," he commanded to Feather before he walked over to meet Raine.

Raine remembered him from Paige's place, but he didn't care about civilities or being cordial. "I'm here to get Feather."

"Hello to you, too. I'm not done interrogating

her."

"Consider yourself done. I'm taking her home."

"No. You aren't. And if you try, I'll have you arrested for obstruction of an investigation. Now, you can wait behind the squad cars with everyone else, and when I am done talking to her, you can take her home."

"Is she under arrest?"

"Not at the moment."

"Are you planning on arresting her?"

"Not sure yet. However, if you don't let me do my job, I'll be more than happy to bring you both to the precinct."

Raine grumbled, glaring at the detective as he crossed his arms in front of his chest. Both men were tall, peering evenly into the other's eyes to see who would blink first. When Raine realized Ren wasn't backing off, he gave in, turning to go back where the general public was gathering to watch.

Satisfied, Ren returned to the car in order to continue his interrogation. He gave Raine another glance and wondered if he was the one who was trying to keep Feather all to himself and eliminating even her girlfriends. In his experience, he was aware of abusive relationships where the man would isolate his partner in order to keep her more suppliant. Could this be the case? He would have to check and see how long the two of them have been a couple and if there were any reports of Raine being abusive. It was only then he realized he did not know Raine's surname.

Ren probably should've taken Feather to the station and asked her the questions there, but he didn't want to leave until after forensic specialists had a chance to go over the scene and get their specimens for testing, or until Shade showed up to take over. He knew both would take awhile, so talking to her here was the best option for the moment.

Feather looked up at his return, her amber eyes deeply concerned. Whiskers sat in her lap as she waited for him to speak first. She couldn't believe she had not recognized him or his scent. Sure, it was almost two hundred years ago, but still, he had made an impression on her with regards to his kindness. She could berate herself for being young and self-centered as all kids were prone to do, yet, she still forgot him. It bothered her that she had been so insensitive to one so kind.

"Sorry about the interruption. So, you say you haven't seen her in years, then out of the blue she contacts you with some important news but has to tell you in person?"

"Yes."

"And you have no idea what the news was about?"

"None. I have no notion of what she might have wanted to tell me. I tried to surmise what it might be over the past couple of days, but nothing came to mind. The best I could come up with was something about either Uxem or Austin, but she could've given me any news about them over the phone. I'm utterly flummoxed by what it might've been."

"What about the third male I met at the train? I don't remember his name. Are you yourself still in contact with them?"

"Payne? He was killed in battle in World War II. The others? Maybe. I've not really been in contact with any of them. Uxem is also dead, but I don't know any more details other than he had passed. Austin, last I heard, is Xulth's apprentice." She paused for a moment. "I'm sorry I didn't remember you. I was and am very grateful for your kindness that first night at the camp."

Ren waved it off. He didn't want her to know his true feelings of disappointment. "It was a long time ago and a couple of lifetimes of experiences in the interim."

"Still, I wanted you to know."

Ren nodded. "Thanks. I don't think I have any more questions at the moment. I have your number when I need more information." He pulled out his wallet and handed her a card. "My number is on here should you think of anything further. Or, if you need anything. Anything at all." It was a subtle indication that if she *was* in trouble or abused, she could call him. She was still a major suspect, but until he was given proof, he would consider her innocent and maybe even a victim in this whole thing. More research into her background, and the other fifteen deaths to see if there was a link to her, would take time.

She took the card and stuck it in her back pocket. "Thanks. I'll keep that in mind. I'm sorry I'm not more help. I want to see this butcher caught and strung up by his toenails. I don't know how much more of this I can take."

"We'll catch him. You can count on that. In the meantime, your ride has been waiting for you."

"Raine? He's here?"

She seemed excited and Ren's heart clenched. He berated himself for caring so much for the person he still couldn't have and barely knew. Sure, they talked all night long, but much in both of their lives had changed over the past couple hundred years. He still couldn't help caring about her and wished he could get to know her better, as well as let her become acquainted with him. He knew she was why he never looked for anyone else after all these years. No one met up to his standards of what he considered when he dreamed about her. He fell for her back at the train station in the foothills of the Guadalupe Mountains and he pined for her ever since. "Yeah." He pointed, then turned and headed back into the house, not wanting to see the loving couple embrace. *She should be mine*, the notion raced through his mind, even though he knew he didn't have the right. *She should be mine. Hopefully, one day, she will be. Raine doesn't look right for her*, he ominously predicted, but then wondered if any guy would look acceptable if that guy wasn't actually himself.

Chapter Six

Raine followed Feather into the house and shut the door behind him. "What the fuck is going on, Spud? And what is up with the cat? We've never wanted pets before."

She couldn't help but smile at his nickname for her. He gave it to her when they were in the boarding school and she had a potato for the first time. She fell in love with them; raw, baked, mashed, every which way they were prepared, she couldn't get enough of them. He teased, saying her face would start to look like a potato spud, and the nickname stuck. No matter the problems or issues they faced, they always seemed to do it together. She couldn't have asked for a better brother than Raine. However, the smile didn't last.

"I don't know, Raine, but it's getting ridiculous. I think Det. Shaw thinks I might be behind their deaths. As for the cat? Her name is Whiskers and she needs a home now that Silver's dead. I'll take care of her. She came to me, sensed my nature, I assume, and I won't abandon her after all of this."

"Yeah, well Shaw's a fucking asshole, as far as I'm concerned."

She didn't say anything. She didn't agree, but she didn't want to tell him about Ren staying with her when she first got to the training camp. Knowing a man stayed in her tipi the first night, even if it was wholly innocent, would set Raine off into a fury she didn't have the energy or inclination to deal with. She was still far too upset over the loss of people she knew, as well as the way they were killed.

"This whole thing is ridiculous. I mean, how many people in the world ever go through the deaths of so many people in unrelated circumstances? I get that we're a bit special over the general humans, that we're blessed by the gods, but still, this? To have them tortured and mutilated?" Feather sat down, burying her head in her hands, Whiskers at her feet. "Had I been on time, I might have found her, just as I did Paige. It's like, whoever is doing this wants me to find them. Like it's a message or something, only I'm not getting what the message is."

"Don't do that to yourself, Spud. Maybe some fucking whack-a-doodle is trying to bait you, and if you keep thinking about it, you'll go insane, or worse, you could've been killed, too. More likely, it's just a major coincidence and nothing more."

"I can only hope, Raine, but I don't know. Something about this, it's just off. I just can't explain it. You know I'm not one for coincidences, and there are far too many here for my liking." She pulled her hands away, folding them in her lap. "Doesn't part of this remind you of what happened back then? I mean, is this a delayed punishment for what happened?"

"No. Nothing would take this long to get its revenge for what happened. Besides, the asshole deserved it."

The asshole Raine was referring to was one of the instructors at the boarding school.

1890

It seemed like yesterday when fourteen-year-old Raine held the hand of twelve-year-old Feather. Several other children of various tribes and ages were also with them. Most were Kiowa, there were several Apache, and the others were not known to him. As a hunter, they were allies with the two he was aware of, but since he had to fend mostly for himself and his sister, he didn't venture too far on the longer trips to give him the education he needed to recognize the kids from the other tribes. Some of the very young clung to whichever older one they knew, terrified of being taken away from their families into unfamiliar and uncertain surroundings. The older ones, especially the boys, appeared defiant, but it was obvious they were scared as well. Some of the girls cried, as did the very young.

Feather huddled closer to Raine, trying to put on a brave face. He could feel her trembling beside him. It didn't help when several stern-looking adults appeared in front of them from the large building situated behind. The older male, with graying hair and mustache, led the others as if they were ducks in a flying formation. When he stopped in front of the group of children, the others stopped behind him.

"Greetings and Salutations. I'm Mister Morgan, the head master. I am fully aware many of you don't understand what I am saying, but you will learn and the ones who have been here already will aid you, as will the other instructors you see behind me.

"There are many rules you will all need to be aware of, and the sooner you learn them, the better off you will be. Each day will be like the other, repetition will help you understand better and learn more efficiently. Today, we will start with giving you Christian names, and for the boys, get your hair cut. Then we will proceed to get you attired in proper civilized clothing. You will forget your heathen ways and learn to take your place in American society. You will only speak English. Any deviation from these rules or any others will get you severely punished.

"All of you will attend Mister Sutter to the fire pit, where the first to go from your old ways will be your hair." He waved to a middle-aged man on his right who stepped up and waved for all of them to follow him. He led them to the front of the building where a large bon fire was already burning. The rest of the adults brought up the rear to make sure no one attempted to stay behind, either because they didn't understand what was being said or were trying to escape. Raine turned his head to watch the proceedings as he and Feather got caught up among the others following Mr. Sutter.

One by one, they were led to one of the older women, Miss White, who held up a pair of scissors. A younger man with the adults took one of the boys closest to the front and brought him towards the woman. He held the boy by his arms, standing in front while the woman cut his hair, throwing the chopped off ponytail into the fire. The children cried out. Some tried to turn and run, others whimpered, unsure what to do to avoid the fate of the boy whose hair was removed. One by one, they were brought to the woman with the scissors to have their hair cut.

Once their hair had been chopped off, another of the women, Miss Lober, took them to have any accoutrements removed, such as their beaded belts, jewelry or feathered gear, as they were also tossed into the fire. Lastly, Mr. Bloom took the boys and Miss Baily took the girls so they could change out of the native clothes they were wearing to put on starched white shirts with high collars and either pants or skirts, respectfully. When they were changed into their new clothing, with or without assistance, the native garments were carried out to the fire and tossed in.

A couple of times the children would speak their language to ask questions, which weren't understood, and one of the adults would hit them and yell, "English only!" It took a while for them to realize they weren't allowed to speak their native tongues. They were being assimilated into the Anglo culture by immersion.

As the children completed preparations for their appearance, Mr. Morgan went through the ranks and gave each child a Christian name to use. Raine was to be called Luke and Feather's new name was Margaret.

One boy was given the name Jacob. He had fought them on the hair issue and was hit and held as they cut it. The adult men had to hold him down as they struggled to change his clothes and they physically struck him with a branch to get him to conform. He would speak his native tongue, they would slap him, but his lack of acceptance of his name was the hardest of all. Payne River wouldn't respond to Jacob no matter how often they called him such or how bad they hit him.

Raine was impressed with Payne's tenacity, despite the fact he also thought the youth extremely foolish to put up with such physical atrocities because he was too stubborn to even pretend to abide them. At least at first. Eventually, Payne, like all the others, accepted his fate on being in the school and learned the ways they were being so diligently taught.

Feather was taught to clean houses and cook, two things she mostly already knew, except the food was different and cleaning also meant dusting. She didn't quite get the concept of that since all it really did was spread the dirt around in the air for a few minutes to resettle back onto whatever it was she dusted.

Their lessons in English, math, reading and writing were done together, which pleased Raine as he could check on his sister, but chores and sleeping were done in different areas. When they had a chance to talk, Feather would comment how she was helping some of the younger girls remain quiet as they cried at night, terrified of what was occurring. She didn't want the matronly women to catch them, for when they did, they were taken out and beaten as punishment. One of the girls had a broken collarbone after being thrown across the room when she upset Mr. Bloom's class by speaking in her native tongue. She couldn't comprehend the answer to a math problem and asked another student for assistance, forgetting to speak English.

Most of the children there, as well as the adults, were humans, but a few were shifters like Raine and Feather. It was the shifters who had the hardest time accepting the religion they were being taught. The Great Spirit made a deal with the spirit guides to protect one group of each tribe, to preserve their existence, their culture, their native tongue and their beliefs. In the time of the gods, the Great Spirit could see the changes about to occur and wished to protect those worthy. One group from each tribe was empowered with the ability to shift into their spirit animal, to have access to the wisdom of their ancestors and to have enhanced animal traits that would guide and protect them. How can the Christian God compete with what the Great Spirit had already accomplished?

The shifters wouldn't come into their powers until puberty, which was usually the time the teens would go on a spirit quest to meet their guide and accept them into their souls to advise and mentor them for the rest of their lives. Raine had a couple of years yet, but Feather was very close to exhibiting power. Raine needed to watch and make sure no one suspected she was more powerful than humans could even contemplate. Yet, while he watched his sister, he couldn't help but watch the other boys as well. In particular, Payne caught his interest and he knew Payne was a shifter. Although he was sure the boy didn't have his powers yet, there was a look of apex predator about him that one shifter recognized in another. Payne was older than Raine. He should be exhibiting powers very soon, but being in the boarding school prevented him and all the others the opportunity to go on the spirit quest.

Raine admitted he was worried about what to do himself and for Feather. Without the sacred ceremony, how would the guides find their human hosts?

Payne was the catalyst that led to Raine and Feather needing to run away. With Feather on the verge of coming into her own powers, Raine needed to make sure his sister was given the opportunity to go on her spirit journey. He would not risk her guide not being able to find her because they were unable to go on the journey all the young needed to take.

Months after their arrival, they completed dinner and their chores were done, as usual. As part of their daily rituals while getting ready for bed, the headmaster came in for nightly prayers. Payne refused to bow down and pray. When Mr. Morgan was about to hit him as punishment, Payne dashed under his arm and down the back stairs. He crawled through the window from the outside staircase and into the girls' room. Feather noticed him immediately. Although she couldn't remember his Indian name, she knew Jacob was one of the chosen, and as a result, refused to succumb to the ways of the white man.

Feather had been huddling with a couple of the youngest in the group, trying to keep them quiet and help them settle down to sleep. She pushed the two girls she was taking care of off to another of the older girls and went over to Jacob. She tried to hide him under a bed before Mr. Morgan, Mr. Bloom and Miss White came into the room looking for Jacob. When the three realized Feather had been hiding him, they took both out of the building for whipping disciplines.

Bloom took Feather off to the back of the barn. She screamed in her head for her brother. There had been many whispered concerns about Bloom getting the girls alone; they were never quite the same when they returned. Subdued, walking slowly in pain, shamed, Bloom did something unspeakable to them. Now he had Feather to punish and he was planning on doing it in private. Feather fought, but a young girl was no match for a full-grown man.

It was the first time Feather communicated with Raine through telepathy. Her fear, co-mingled with her budding puberty, allowed her to call him. *Raine! Raine! I need help. Bloom is going to hurt me. No! No! He is hurting me. Stop! Make him stop! Raine! Brother, I need you!*

Raine was shocked at the voice suddenly in his

head. Only a handful could communicate telepathically, and although most were siblings, it was still very rare, especially in those who were pre-pubescent. He ran to the window to see Bloom pulling Feather to the barn where some of the animals were kept. He checked to make sure no one saw him, then slipped out the window to the ground below, running to the barn to save his sister from whatever evil Bloom had in mind.

Feather was squirming, trying to get away, terror coursing through her veins. Of all the instructors at the school, Bloom had a reputation of being the cruelest. He pulled her inside one of the stalls and proceeded to lift her skirt up and pull down her bloomers. He whacked her hard on her bottom with one hand while he held her small form around her waist with the other. He wacked her a couple of more times while the hand holding her moved up to her budding breasts. She screamed, but he didn't care. The others were out looking for Jacob. Margaret, aka Feather, was his to punish. He grabbed a broken bottle in the stall, about to push the sharp edges against her perfect skin, when Raine rushed in and called for his sister.

He shook with anger when he saw the state Feather was in, her tear-stained face, her skirt up exposing her deeply red buttocks. Raine saw the glass's sharp edges Bloom was about to inflict on her privates. Raine was fairly positive Bloom planned to cut her had he not intruded. He ran towards Bloom, fury and hatred in his eyes. Raine had also been exposed to Bloom's cruel punishments in the past, such as when he would talk to his sister in their native language or not respond to the name they gave him, as well as other multiple infractions he wasn't even entirely sure of.

Bloom would take him to a post outside and spank him with his belt, stopping just short of breaking the skin. Another time, he forced Raine to crawl on all fours for hours, scraping his knees to the point of being horribly bruised before he was once again allowed to stand.

As he ran towards Bloom, a funny, strange feeling came over him. It was slightly painful, but not enough to cause him to stop his attack. Yet, when he looked down at his hands as he leapt at the male, he didn't see fingers but claws, and his arms were covered with a tawny fur. He didn't care. His focus was on protecting his sister, not the first time he shifted, his spirit guide coming to the forefront as if the guide knew this was the moment to reveal himself instead of waiting for an official ritual. Raine's jaws clamped down on Bloom's arm holding the glass and blood sprayed into Raine's mouth.

Bloom held up his arm defensively as he wailed with a high-pitched scream. Raine didn't care. His new-found animal instincts took over and he willingly gave into them. He used his claws to slash across Bloom's face, his sharp nails catching Bloom's eyeball and pulling it loose from its socket. Raine clawed in rapid succession, leaving behind a multitude of inflictions across his chest, face and legs. Blood poured swiftly down Bloom's body, the deep-red liquid pooling around the now-quiet, unmoving body. Only when Bloom stopped moving did Raine back off and look around for Feather to ensure she was okay.

Feather had used the distraction to move out of the way and pull up her bloomers. The material rubbed against her raw behind, but she ignored the soreness as she watched with abject fascination at her brother's new form. Grateful, amazed, stunned surprise intermingled with the viciousness of her brother's assault.

The cougar, also known as a mountain lion, which was her brother, turned and came towards her. She reached out carefully, trusting Raine to not hurt her. After all, he just saved her and he was still her brother. Raine's fur was covered in red, so he only used the top of his head to rub against her hand. They both looked up as sounds of approaching adults headed their way. Then they heard Payne calling to them from a hole located at the back of the barn. By going through the opening, they could follow him away from the structure.

Raine headed towards the hole; Feather followed him. Raine moved to the side and waited until Feather was able to step through the rotted opening. He was pretty sure in his new-found lion guise he wouldn't fit. He also wasn't sure how to shift back into his human form. He tried but failed while Feather was crawling through.

Payne must've realized the problem and, once Feather was free of the barn, pushed her towards the safety of a line of trees. Then, Payne sat on his ass and used his feet to kick the rotted planks off so the cougar would fit. When they knew the coast was clear, they both ran towards the tree line.

Once they got to the edge of the forest, Payne pushed Raine towards his sister. "Go towards the now-set sun. I'll get them to follow me in the opposite direction. They won't realize you're even missing for hours since they will be too busy chasing me."

Raine and Feather exchanged a silent look between them. Since Raine was still a lion, Feather spoke, seeming to know what Raine would've said if he were able to speak.

"Are you sure? It's dangerous. What if they

catch you?"

"They won't. You need the chance to get away. Now go. There's not much time!"

Feather moved to Payne and hugged him. "Thank you. From both of us."

The siblings took off. Payne waited for a moment to watch, then turned back towards the school.

Turning back to make sure they were not noticed, they spotted an owl flying over the barn. Moments later, the barn was ablaze. Bloom would probably be discovered, but no one would know it was Raine, or even a lion, that ended Bloom's life.

Present

As Feather reached down to pet Whiskers, she realized Raine made a valid point. It wouldn't take over two hundred years for revenge to be taken for Bloom's death. It just wasn't logical, despite all the oddness the world had to offer, including the magical powers gifted to certain tribes.

Still, Feather couldn't get the idea out of her mind that the loss of Silver and Paige were a consequence of Bloom's death. The idea mostly revolved around the eyes being taken out and the burning of the body.

Raine pulled her around to face him. "It's not a punishment for that asshole. Whoever's doing this, he'll be caught and you'll be safe."

"I hope you're right, bro. I hope you're right."

Chapter Seven

Shaw sat at his desk looking over all the reports that had been coming in the past couple of days from Redmond's murder. He was fairly certain Swimming Otter's would yield similar information, unless the perp made a mistake. Ren highly doubted that would be an occurrence, although he could hope. The murderer was too meticulous, from what he could discern thus far. From the criminologists, to forensics experts, to entomologists and the pathologists, all had some interesting information. The eyes were gouged out with what looked like sharp claws or talons. The main organs, or at least those that were left inside, appeared to have aged more rapidly than the rest of the body. There were no defensive wounds, and nothing under the nails of the victims, so it seemed the women didn't fight back, or didn't have the opportunity to. Mostly likely they were so surprised by their attacker they didn't have much of a chance.

Detective Apple Shade sat across from Ren

with another file. "The toxicology report is a dead end. Nothing to indicate what might have attacked them. Did you read the bit about their eyes being gouged out by claws or talons? What? Did they train a hawk to pluck out people's pupils? Hah. Say that five times fast. Pluck people's pupils."

She had spent her time with the forensics team doing some of the other leg work and phone calls while Shaw had been with the witness, Feather Woods.

"I doubt it, Shade. More like a folklore, a myth coming to light."

She gave him a dubious look. "Really, Shaw. All these years, I never took you for being fanciful."

"I'm not. I'm looking at the facts. Besides, there is a bit of truth in all myths." He gave her a pointed look. "You know what our kind is capable of."

Yeah, she knew all too well. They were both Kiowa Spirit Walkers. Apple was a deer, protector of the Earth and one who sacrifices for the people, things she had done all her life inherently before being gifted with these attributes. Becoming a police officer seemed the natural step for her. What surprised many was her tenacity and inner strength. Albeit, she never quite understood why. After all, sacrificing for the general good took intense strength and perseverance.

Apple looked at the reports again, particularly the wounds in the chest cavity and the eyes. "Why do you think he is burning the bodies? To hide possible trace evidence?"

"Could be. Or it could be something else. This is one time I almost wish I were a profiler. I have no idea, even after all these years, why some nut jobs do the things they do. Sadly, I know there is usually a reason, but fuck me if I can ever figure it out." He tossed Apple another stack of files. "Sixteen known cases. *Sixteen*. And no one has put them together before. Not even as a copycat. I get that the human world doesn't understand about us or our longevity, but shit, Shade, are they that fucking blind?"

"When it comes to things that can't be explained? Yeah, they are. Better to ignore it if there is no reasonable explanation."

"What happened to, 'Once you eliminate the impossible, whatever remains, no matter how improbable, must be the truth'?"

"Sherlock Holmes is dead?" Shade quipped back. "Mostly likely, it's easier to make up or ignore the impossible and improbable. Humans are good at ignoring things right under their own noses if they don't want to believe." Apple shook her head. "So now what? Should we go talk to Ms. Woods again? Or the employers and co-workers of the latest two vics?"

Ren would love a chance to go talk to Feather again, but he realized he needed to talk to the others as well. "We should split the assignments. I'll deal with Ms. Redmond's friends and co-workers and see if they know anything. You deal with Swimming Otter's associates. We can compare notes later to see if they have a commonality."

"And the other fourteen? Some of them are going to be impossible to find since they died forty and fifty years ago, and were humans. I'm actually surprised we even know about them considering the lack of technology and all back then."

"True. Someone got bored and scanned the reports into the mainframe database. Lucky us. However, that also means these murders could date back even further, there are just no records of it for us to pick up as a nationwide search."

Apple put the file down and leaned over conspiratorially. "What if we follow a different trail?"

Ren's curiosity was piqued. "How so?"

Apple plopped a file down in front of him. When he opened it, he saw the notes he made on Feather. "Let's follow her past and see how many of the people we know about knew her. If my hunch is right, we can follow her history back even further to find more, and maybe even the person who is behind it, as well as a motive."

"You think she is the motive?" Ren scanned over his notes again. It was true, both of the latest victims knew her. Both had met or were planning on meeting with her prior to their demise. And, both were now deceased in the same manner. Apple could be on to something.

"I think it's worth looking into. Hell, she might even be the culprit and a good actress."

Ren would hate to think so, but it certainly wasn't a possibility he could automatically refute, especially since he had thought the same idea himself. "Let's get the easy leg work done and then focus on the background of Ms. Woods."

Chapter Eight

Apple entered the bar and headed right for the bartender. She flashed her badge and asked to speak to the manager.

"Ain't here," the thin, gum-chewing, bald man replied as he made a show of using a towel to dry a glass he held in his hands.

Apple frowned and pulled out a picture of Silver. "This woman was in here yesterday. Do you recognize her?"

"I didn't work yesterday." He popped a bubble and looked bored with the whole conversation, not even looking at the picture.

"Who was working then?"

The man shrugged.

She turned around and addressed the few that were in the bar: a couple of burly men in the back corner and an old man sitting at a table reading a newspaper as he sipped a beer. He had caught her attention when the bartender said he wasn't working yesterday and it planted the idea the bartender was lying. There was also a couple talking quietly, huddled in a back booth. It was relatively early, so the bar was still fairly empty. She took the picture and moved to the table with the old man, putting it in front of his paper so he had to see it.

"Have you seen this woman in here?"

The man grumbled a no, shifting the paper to the side so he could continue reading.

Throwing another look at the obstinate bartender, she moved over to the burly men. They both stood up and met her halfway. They both towered over her as they neared her. She could smell the alcohol on their breaths as they approached, but they seemed fairly steady so they probably only had a couple of beers and weren't intoxicated too heavily.

She held the picture out to them. "Have you seen this woman?"

The taller of the two glanced at it, then pulled it from her fingers for an even closer look. "Hey, Bud. Isn't this the woman you did the other day?" He passed the picture to the guy behind him and moved closer to Apple. "Now me, you're more my type. What say you?"

"I say, I'm not interested in your advances, but if you really did see this woman, then I am interested in that."

"Nah, she weren't my type," Bud replied, but held onto the picture.

The bigger man stepped closer to Apple and touched her hair. "You might be if ya knew what you were missing."

She stepped closer and, before he realized it, her nails dug into his balls and he was on his knees in pain with her leaning over him. "As I said, I'm not interested. I suggest you leave me alone, or next time, I'll pull your balls off and stuff them down that gaping hole you call a mouth. Got it?"

The guy whimpered and nodded. His friend cupped his private area and nodded as well. She didn't let go, but looked around to make sure any and all who thought otherwise considered different ideas. When she was sure she made her point, she let him go and pushed him to the side, moving around him to Bud and snagged the picture back.

She returned to the bartender and slapped the picture down. "Let me try this again. I hate being lied to and I have a very distinct feeling you were working here yesterday. In fact, I have a pretty good notion you work here every day and are the owner of the establishment, since the name on your shirt matches the first name of the liquor license you have on the wall behind you. So, I repeat, have you seen this woman?"

The bartender was pale as he watched the altercation between the men and her. Shakily, he gave the picture a closer look. "Yeah. She was in here last night. Didn't stay very long and ain't a regular. She had a couple of beers by herself, then left."

"Did anyone follow her out?"

"No. As I said she was by herself the entire time and remained that way, as far as I could tell, when she left."

"What time would you say she was here?"

"From about 5 to 7:30."

"Thank you." Det. Shade grabbed the picture and left the establishment.

Once she was back in her car, she pulled out her notepad and jotted down the pertinent information. So far, she had the time line of Silver Swimming Otter. And from what appeared in her investigation, Silver's routine didn't change much from day to day. Yesterday varied slightly with the addition of the bar instead of her normal restaurant. Her co-workers said she seemed a bit more agitated throughout the day, checking the clock often. One of her colleagues mentioned Silver told her she was planning on meeting a friend she had not seen in a long time and she was nervous about it.

Yesterday, Silver went to work as a file clerk from 8:30 to 4:30, drove to the bar and was there from 5 to 7:30. She had no interactions with anyone in particular. Nothing out of the ordinary. No Stalkers. No surprise visitors. Silver's life was almost as boring as her own. All work and little-to-no play. Few friends, and the one she had a meeting with today was Feather Woods. The more she thought about it, the more Shade wanted to go with her gut. Feather was the culprit behind all of these deaths. Now, she just had to convince her partner and prove it.

Chapter Nine

1941

Raine looked at Payne, astonishment clearly on his face. "You what?"

Payne appeared extremely uncomfortable all of a sudden. "I want to claim Feather as my own."

Raine scrubbed his face. He had known Payne for over fifty years, having first met him at the boarding school they had been shipped off to when Raine was only fourteen. Payne, who was a year older, arrived shortly after. During those brief years, Raine grew relatively close to the older boy, intrigued by Payne's constant rebellion against the rules the school tried to institute.

Raine didn't think he even knew Feather existed at that time, until the night Raine killed Bloom for molesting Feather. To help with their escape, Payne had led the administrators away, and in the process set the barn on fire, destroying all evidence of Bloom's demise by Raine's attack.

They lost contact after they escaped that night, each going their own way. It was several years later before the two men crossed paths again. The next time Raine saw Payne, he was headed to the Guadalupe Mountains.

1897

Raine sat on his Mustang, looking in the distance to the tall range in Texas. It would be the first time in a couple of years since he last saw his sister board a train to come to this area. He had missed her greatly, but it had been her destiny not his. True, they had all been blessed with the gifts bestowed onto them by the Great Spirit, but there were some within the tribes who were more favored than others. Some whose powers were stronger, more significant than the rest, and thereby needed special training. Feather was one of those who had been endowed with enhanced gifts. As a result, she was sent to learn how to handle her new and growing powers with the medicine man, Xulth. She would acquire the skills needed to focus her new abilities and harness the power so not to accidentally expose humans to the talents some natives were endowed with.

Five years. He had not seen her in five years and Raine had to wonder how she had changed, how she had grown. She was still a child in a way when she left at the age of fourteen. A young woman just beginning to blossom. What kind of woman would be waiting for him at the Sun Dance Ceremony, which also served as a kind of graduation for those who were trained by Xulth?

The Sun Dance Ceremony was usually close to the Medicine Lodge and was to establish and maintain kinship with all the people's relatives, including those who were not only human, but also related to the animals and plants of the Earth, as well as the cosmic relatives of the Spirit Realm. For the human Native American tribes, they would need to do some sort of self-sacrifice and fasting to gain visions for their supernatural aid. But for those who were blessed with the powers to shift into their spirit guides, with all the abilities attributed to their animal counterpart, self-sacrifice was unnecessary, as was the need to abstain for visions of the supernatural. However, they usually refrained from eating in order to cleanse the body of darkness and impurities, a need they had felt more important since the arrival of the Europeans and the diseases they brought.

Sun Dances had diminished greatly over the last couple of years, ever since the attack at Wounded Knee in 1890 in response to the Ghost Dances, which were similar to the Sun Dance with a few variations. With the Ghost Dance, the religious belief of the destruction of Earth would occur and a new world would be born. This new world would be abundant with game and deceased relatives, and best of all, no Anglo-Saxons. The gathering for the Ghost Dance made U.S. soldiers and American settlers nervous. They feared the assembly of so many Native Americans would lead to an armed attack against them. A misunderstanding, taut nerves, a deaf man who didn't hear the orders to disarm, a weapon's discharge and all hell broke loose, leaving many dead, including several women and children. As a consequence, most of the gatherings for ceremonial dances had been outlawed. It was only because this Sun Dance was held in secret that they were able to continue the ceremonious tradition.

Raine kicked his horse back into moving, a slow gait, for there was no hurry to arrive as the ceremony was still two days away and he had, at best, only a day's ride left. A part of him hoped he would be able to see Feather beforehand, but he was unsure what the procedures were with regards to the possibility. He would set up camp in the foothills of the mountains and then proceed up to the lodge tomorrow. Surely, he would not be the only one arriving early.

When he made camp later that night, he felt eyes watching him. He may have been an easy target as a human, but in his spirit form he was much more formidable. He didn't need to shift in order to access the senses he obtained from his guide. He lifted his nose into the air and sniffed. With his keen sense of smell, as well as the exceptional eyesight of a feline, he scanned the area around him. Only an owl in the tree above watched him.

Raine became fearful. Owls were evil omens, usually symbolizing death. As a child, his mother would often relate to him and Feather stories warning the children to remain inside at night and not cry too much or the owl would come and carry them away, never to be seen again. The owls would suck the soul and life right out of a person. Even adults were not immune, and owls would serve as a warning to those who broke tribal law.

As a mountain lion, the personification of power, grace, strength, speed and agility, the idea that an owl was what he feared had him almost laughing at the absurdity of it. Why should he be nervous about a simple bird? He would have laughed, too, if he weren't so frightened of the damned thing. It was then the owl flew towards his head. Raine yelped, ducking as he covered his head.

Laughter had him peeking through his arms. When he saw Payne, he stood upright and looked around for the owl before turning his attention back to his visitor. "You?"

Payne nodded, still laughing slightly. "Yeah."

Raine folded his arms in aggravation. "Really? That was you?"

Payne nodded again, his laughter subsiding slightly. "Yeah. Lucky me, I get a guide who is the personification of death." He lunged with his arms upraised, his hands clawed. "Boo!" Then he laughed again as Raine jumped back slightly. "I figured you'd be coming. Thought I'd meet up with you."

Raine ignored him for a moment, gathering wood to build a fire and calm down from his momentary fright. "Who are you coming to see at the center?"

Payne realized what he was doing, moving to assist with some of the logs. "No one. I'm one of the students."

Raine glanced back at that tidbit of news.

"You?" Then he thought about it for a minute. When he knew Payne at the boarding school, he had thought Payne had shown some powers early on, but he wasn't positive about it. He just hadn't given it much credibility until now. "Yep. I guess I can see that."

"Don't need to sound so surprised, you know."

"I know. I'm sorry. Just caught me off guard." Raine finished putting together a small stack of wood in which to start a fire. He used his own powers to light the bundle, a small blaze from the tips of his fingers shot out to ignite the logs. The warmth quickly spread around the circle of flame as both Raine and Payne sat on the ground near it.

"Feather trained very well. She did your family proud."

Raine tilted his head in acknowledgment. "I had little doubt. I'm sure you did your family just as proud."

"I don't have any. My mother died in childbirth. My father with the white man's disease."

"I didn't know."

Payne shrugged. "It's old news and they're both in a better place. They passed before giving me siblings, so I'm used to being on my own."

"Still. I don't know what I would do if I didn't have my sister."

"I remember you once telling me your mother had passed. You didn't talk about your father and neither does Feather."

Raine nodded. "Mother had an accident. She fell into our fire and was severely burned. She continued to live for a couple of years afterwards, but she never recovered and eventually joined our ancestors on the other side."

"And your father?"

"He still lives."

Payne raised his eyebrow at the comment. "I take it you don't like him?"

"I give him the respect he deserves as my father, but little else. He has been consumed with white man's firewater and has done little in caring for my sister and I."

This time, Payne nodded in understanding.

"That explains Feather's reluctance to discuss her family outside of you. Nemene are usually very good to their children, as they are the future. In return, the children are very good to the elders, as they earned the wisdom. Without that balance between the two, life is more difficult."

"Yeah. It's been a challenge. Father would not let the village know of our plight and we were forbidden to associate with the elders. After Mother's demise, my grandfather passed from a broken heart and my training ceased. I picked up the mantle in caring for Feather, protecting her as best as I could."

"You're only two revolving suns older?"

"Yes."

"For one so young, it must have been hard to take on the mantle of raising her."

"Not really. She was aware of the situation and of my plight. She was always respectful and appreciative of what I needed to do for the two of us. Of all things, she most likely hated that I left her alone to come here. I didn't have a choice, though.

The Elders felt it was necessary with her promising abilities. She far surpassed me and anything I could teach her."

"She didn't, you know. Resent you. I know she was grateful for coming here to learn. She missed you, don't get me wrong, but she also knew this was where she needed to be."

"And you, Payne. How did you fair?"

"I learned my strengths as well as my weaknesses. I gained the knowledge needed to temper my powers and use them wisely. Xulth is a great master in that respect. You will be proud of your sister."

"I've always been proud of her."

* * *

Learning of Payne's lack of family encouraged Raine to invite Payne to accompany Feather and himself back to their village once the Sun Dance Ceremony was completed. A part of him wondered what his father would say, but then his father had been around less and less over the past few years. It was about three days before Storm even realized Payne was there and he wasn't Raine.

About a week after that, Storm came back to the abode worse than Raine had seen him in quite a while, and that was saying a lot. He wasn't exactly sure what the particular offense was, but Storm physically went after Feather. He had known in the past not to even try his macho bull with Raine, the younger man could more than defend himself against the drunken older male. However, Feather had been gone the few years prior, and he didn't consider how her powers were now at full strength and she could squash him like a bug with barely a second thought. Yet, Feather always had a gentle soul and she would never abuse her power like that.

Regardless, Raine was not about let him abuse his sister, regardless of whether or not she could fend for herself.

As Raine and Payne came back from hunting, they entered to find Storm over Feather with his hand raised threateningly. Raine didn't think, didn't hesitate. He barreled into Storm, knocking him away from his sister, punching him in the face. He was sure his father was down for the count, so he left Storm's prone body to check on Feather. His back was to Storm and Payne as his focus was on his sister, who was saying she was okay and that Storm caught her by surprise.

When they heard a cry, Raine spun around ready to meet the danger head on. What he didn't expect was to see Payne standing over a prone Storm with a bloodied knife. Payne didn't look apologetic or remorseful in any way as he held the dripping blade and leaned down ready to scalp him.

"No!" Feather called out in horror. "Don't. Please."

"What happened?" Raine growled as he moved over to the remains of his father.

Payne stopped and stood. "He was going to attack you from behind. He has abused you long enough and I ended it. You both will be safe from now on." He held the knife out to Raine. "Do you wish to accept the power of taking his scalp for yourself? I will not deny you that right."

Raine grasped the knife, just to get it away from Payne. "There is no pride in taking the power of one such as him. Nor will I allow anyone else to take it. He did not have to be killed."

Payne growled. "Yes, he did. Look." Payne nudged Storm with his foot, moving him just enough out of the way in order to see a large knife under him.

Raine's eyes narrowed. After all this time, he never thought his father would have the guts to try and kill his offspring, but he guessed his assumptions were incorrect. The blade glinted in the firelight of the structure. Raine turned and grabbed Feather by her arm headed towards the entryway. Payne automatically followed them, surprised when Raine pushed Feather into his arms. "Take her away from the village. I need to take care of this and I don't want either of you accidentally implicated."

Payne hesitated a moment. Then, taking Feather's arm, pulled her outside to the horses. He literally threw her on the back of the horse and climbed on behind her before she could protest, urging the horse to a gallop from the village.

Once Raine knew they were safely away, he turned back and looked around again. He grabbed a few items, things he knew Feather would want or he, himself, desired. He threw them into a small bag and took another look around, his eyes landing on the still form of his father. Storm's eyes were open, staring lifelessly towards Raine. The windows to the soul and nothing was left remaining to gaze upon. Raine almost felt a chill go through him as he stared into the cold, exanimate orbs, almost feeling as if he were being judged from beyond for what he was about to do. Raine had to protect his friend and his sister from the darkness of this event. He couldn't risk the stain on Payne's soul for wanting to save him and, in the process, Feather. No, this was on Raine.

The current tradition was to wrap the body in blankets and tie him behind a horse, where the body would be ridden to an appropriate burial site. The rider would cover the body with stones in a secure location, usually inside a cave or buried under a tree. All the deceased items would then be burned as part of the ceremony. Raine would skip the burying part and burn the body and the items together. Get rid of the middleman, so to speak. They would also forgo the slicing of the arms and body for the loss of a loved one. Raine realized neither he nor Feather loved Storm. He was their parent, and as such, accorded him the respect due to one in such a role, but Storm lost any love his children had for him the moment his drunken anger issues rose. They were increased by their mother's burning and subsequent death, as well as the abuse the children suffered at Storm's hands.

Glaring one last time into Storm's empty eyes, he turned and used his powers to light the structure on fire. Escaping quickly, he galloped into the forest to meet up with Payne and Feather knowing none of them could return to the village he had known since birth.

1941

Raine stood there, the shock as Payne asked for Feather as his mate clearly palpable. Granted, Kiowas and Comanches were allies, so uniting the two wouldn't be an issue in that regard. However, as Payne had remained with them for decades, he became more like a brother than a potential suitor for Feather. And this coming just before they headed off to war? Talk about poor timing. What was he supposed to do, say yes and hope everything went okay as they headed off to Europe to fight the Nazis? Tell him to wait and see when they returned?

"I'll need to talk to Feather. This kind of decision she should have a say in. She might say no, because of the war and all."

"That is her choice, but if you don't say no, she won't. You're not saying no, are you?"

Hell, yes. I'm saying no. The words screamed in his head, but he said nothing of the sort out loud. "I'll talk to Feather. The decision will be hers and I will abide by whatever decision she makes."

Raine realized he should have said no, taking the consequences, but Payne had been his friend, his blood brother. Too many years, too many adventures had been shared between the two of them to want to hurt him by refusing the proposal outright. Yeah. He was a chicken shit. He hoped he could delay the talk so the war became the uppermost thing in their minds and the thought of marrying his baby sister fell to the wayside. After the war was over, then they could broach the subject.

The two men were supposed to leave for basic training in a couple of weeks anyways. It shouldn't be too hard to keep the subject away from marriage. There was just something about Payne that bothered Raine, and he sensed it bothered Feather as well. Over the past few decades, Payne's cruelness showed through. He was ruthless, vicious and merciless as they fought side by side. Raine often thought he was glad he was an ally instead of an enemy, for he would not wish to go against Payne at any time. True, Raine could also be sadistic when warranted, but with Payne, he seemed to get a bit too much enjoyment out of it. More so than seemed appropriate. As a result, he didn't want his sister to marry him. Maybe a part of him was afraid that brutish behavior would turn against her, like his father had to Suni. He wasn't willing to take that chance, not where Feather was concerned.

How quickly that time flew. One minute they were talking about whether or not Raine would give permission to Payne to ask Feather to marry him, the next they were getting ready to ship out. Raine and Payne did not remain together, each going into different areas of the service. Raine ended up working as a Comanche code talker, which was originally formed back in World War I but hadn't really progressed into an organized efficient code until it was developed in World War II. Similar to the more famous Navajo code talkers, there were twenty-one Comanche men who were part of the program.

Payne, on the other hand, was part of the Army Infantry. Since Payne had no other family than

Raine and Feather, it was Feather who got the telegram from the government with regards to Payne's demise. It seemed he was part of what was known as the Battle of the Bulge, a term coined by the press to describe the bulge in Allied front lines on wartime maps. The Allies originally called it the Ardennes counter offensive. The Germans hoped to stop the Allied use of a Belgian port called Antwerp, and thereby split the Allied lines of defense, which would allow the Germans to circle and attack. Hitler believed he could fully concentrate on the Eastern Front and the Soviets once this offensive was accomplished. Raine and others sent word to the Allies of the impending attack, but nothing was acted upon by the Allies to prevent it. When all was said and done, over 80,000 U.S. men had perished. Payne was listed among those killed and Raine never had to let Feather know about Payne's interest in making Feather his wife.

Chapter Ten

Present

Apple and Ren finished up their current interviews with each of the victim's friends and family, adding little or no additional leads in either of the two cases. Although there were still quite a lot of items to comb through for leads from both women, so far, the only thing apparent was having Feather Woods as a mutual acquaintance. They either saw or talked to her recently. There didn't appear to be any other noticeable common denominator between the two victims.

Worse, as they delved more into the backgrounds of the other fourteen victims since 1948 who matched the horrific demise of Paige and Silver, somehow, in one way or another, Feather Woods knew them. Some it appeared casually, others a bit more intimately. After hours of tedious work, Apple looked up at Ren from across her desk. "As much as I hate to say this, I think it's time we bring in Ms. Woods for interrogation on all of these crimes."

"It's just so rare to have a female serial killer this depraved and ferocious. The gouging of the heart from the chest cavity, the clawing out of the eyes, the burning of the bodies. There was no need for the latter back in the 1940s until the 1980s as forensic analyses had not been as modern as today. Which is why most of these commonalities were overlooked within the system."

"It's not unheard of, though. Female serial killers. Hell, Bobbitt cut off her husband's penis. That's pretty messed up. And Charlene Gallego raped and murdered teenage girls very sadistically in 1980. Or 1982's Judith Neelley, who liked to torture her teenage victims. Or my personal favorite, Juana La Peque Sicaria, who was the executioner for the Los Zetas cartel. She was involved in multiple decapitations, as well as confessed to using severed body parts as sexual stimulants in 2016. There may not be as many, but the women serial killers out there are just as vicious and ruthless as the men. There're even some who were cannibals. Feather Woods sounds just as depraved as the ones I mentioned. A complete sociopath, and considering what she is, I see no issues at all making her our prime suspect."

Ren pinched the bridge of his nose with his thumb and forefinger. He knew Apple was right in her concerns, but he still remembered the Feather he met at the train station who was so young and innocent, excited for her first time riding the Iron Horse. He liked her then and he found those feelings hadn't changed much over the century since. It wasn't until he saw her at Paige Redmond's place that he realized how much he still thought about this woman over the years. He just couldn't believe she was behind all of the murders, but then, he really didn't know her anymore and people change. The one main question he had was what changed her? What was the one pivotal event that occurred to set her on the path of destroying so many lives? What was the catalyst that pushed her to kill? Additionally, why take the eyes? Why take the heart? What did she do with them? And why did the insides of the victims appear to have aged more so than the outsides? He knew Det. Shade was correct, and the only way they were going to get any clear answers was to bring Feather Woods in as a person of interest in the murders of Paige Redmond and Silver Swimming Otter.

"Do we want to treat her as a person of interest or get a warrant for her arrest?"

Shade thought about it for a minute. "How about we bring her in as a person of interest? Depending on her answers, we can arrest her on the spot, if need be. Besides, we would need more physical evidence to get a warrant. What we have now wouldn't fill a cavity."

"Alright, let's go. I'll tell the Captain what we have so far and meet you at the car."

"What are you going to say about the older cases? Woman does not look old enough to have done the 1948 murder or the ones shortly thereafter."

"We are going to focus on the ones from 1990

and, in particular, the most current crimes, which she could have feasibly committed. If we can prove those to the humans, we can show the older ones to the Tribal Elders."

"I hate working for two factions like this."

"I know, Shade. But they can't know about our kind, our powers, our gifts. They would never understand, and I personally don't want to be put under a microscope to be studied for all eternity."

"I get it, Shaw. I do. But I really hate it."

"Agreed. There are many times I do as well."

Chapter Eleven

Detectives Shade and Shaw stood at the door, badges in hand when Feather opened it. She smiled slightly, her eyes rimmed in red from recently crying. Feather ushered them into the kitchen and offered them coffee. For the moment, Ren and Apple decided to keep her comfortable to answer their questions. If the interrogation didn't provide adequate results, they could always bring her downtown later. She grabbed a couple of mugs out of the cupboard and poured them each some coffee, putting cream and sugar on the table.

"We need to go over some of the information we got from you earlier, if you don't mind." Ren pulled out his notebook and pen. He had to look away. She was so beautiful, he couldn't concentrate otherwise. An inner part of him really wanted Feather to be innocent and the whole thing just a major coincidence. A stalker or a random sociopath would be much more preferable than having her as a murdering, cannibalistic criminal.

"Sure. Whatever you need. Do you have a suspect yet? Anything to help find whoever did that to my friends."

Shade wasn't as successful as acting so nonchalant as Ren was. She felt Feather was guilty as sin and didn't even try to hide her contempt. Feather gave her one look, then focused on Ren. She could sense the antagonism the female detective was emitting. Albeit, she was unsure why.

"Tell us again, the last time you saw or spoke to Ms. Redmond."

"It was a couple of weeks ago. We had a stupid fight—argument. We hadn't spoken in days and I went over to see her that morning when I…I found her." She stood and moved to a box of tissues on the counter. "Sorry. I still can't quite get over seeing her that way. Of finding her dead like that. Who could do such a thing?"

Ren locked eyes with Apple and shook his head, warning her against saying anything. He knew Apple all too well, and with a question posed like that, he was pretty positive she would answer the question with a "You." They couldn't afford that kind of response, now, if they were ever going to get her to answer all of their questions. Currently, she was unaware of what they suspected, or how far back the murders went. They needed to keep it that way in order to get as much information out of her as possible.

Apple rolled her eyes, totally expecting the warning. She was not a rookie and knew better in keeping her mouth shut with her own snide comments and opinions. Instead, she brought the coffee mug to her mouth in order to keep it busy.

"Did she or anyone else know you were going to see her that morning?"

Feather fingered the tissue in her hand as she thought about it. "I mentioned it to Raine that I hated the rift between us. I said I might go over and talk to her. It was such a silly, stupid misunderstanding."

Shaw scribbled down furiously in his note pad. Yes, he was really beginning to like Raine as the primary suspect. A jealous, controlling suitor who'd want her all to himself. He might even be abusive. "Have you been with Raine for a long time?"

Feather smiled wistfully. "All my life."

Fuck! Ren thought. *She was truly in love and he may be a dangerous monster.*

"And Ms. Swimming Otter?"

Feather blew her nose and tossed the tissue away, bringing the box back with her to the table as she sat back down. "Silver?" She tried to think. "I guess the last time I saw her was about six years ago, at Uxem's services. You might remember, he was one of our fellow colleagues from training in the mountains with Xulth."

"How did he die?" Shade kept the mug between her hands knowing Shaw was taking all the notes from the inquiries.

Feather had to think about it for a moment. "Honestly, I'm not really sure. It was more of a memorial ceremony than a funeral."

"How did you find out about his death?" Ren scribbled away furiously in his note pad.

"Austin, another of our colleagues, sent word

out to the four of us."

"Were there not four plus you brought to the camp?"

"Yes, but one of them, Payne River, was killed in action at the Battle of the Bulge in 1945."

"And how did Austin know?"

Feather gave a slight shrug of her shoulders. "I assume Xulth. He had a way of getting messages of who crossed over. He connected with them as he did during our education."

"Why would Xulth contact Austin first? Why didn't he contact you himself?"

"Probably because Austin is his apprentice."

Ren raised his eyes from his pad for the first time since he started the questioning. "I was unaware of that."

"After the second war, Austin wanted to go back to more of the traditional ways. The world was changing too fast for him, so he headed back to the Guadalupe Mountains to convince Xulth to train him to be a teacher. He has been there ever since."

"Could Uxem have been murdered like Paige

and Silver?"

"If he was, I wasn't aware of it. They really didn't disclose how he died, or maybe we just didn't want to know. The loss of one of our own is hard to accept, especially when one was as powerful as Uxem."

"When is the last time you talked to Silver?"

"A couple of days ago; she called me. It was kind of an unexpected surprise."

"What did she call you about?"

Feather shook her head. "As I mentioned before, I don't know. She wouldn't say over the phone. Said we had to meet in person."

"And she gave no indication as to what it might be in reference to?"

"None. She only said she couldn't tell me over the phone. We had to meet face to face and we made arrangements to meet at her house at 10 a.m."

Ren was quiet as he made a few more notes. He then pulled out some of the previous notes regarding the other fourteen deaths.

"Do you know a Linda Mahoney?"

Feather blinked in surprise. "Um. Yeah. She was my old boss when I worked at a fast food place in Kansas a few years back. Why are you asking about her?"

"When is the last time you saw her?"

"The day I quit and left Chucky's Chicken Shack. Again, why are you asking about her?"

"When was that?"

"Um. I left Kansas in 2007 and I quit just a few months prior, so I guess November 2006?"

"Can you be more specific?"

"Why?"

Shade injected disdainfully, "Please just answer the questions, Ms. Woods. Det. Shaw and I will make everything known to you once you have competed answering everything."

Feather gave the woman a glance. She had been quiet for the most part up until now, since Ren had been leading the inquiries. Feather took a deep breath and nodded. "I know it was before the holidays but a couple of weeks after Halloween. So, I would estimate the last time I saw her was maybe the fourteenth or fifteenth? I'm sorry, I don't think I can narrow it down any more than that. It was a few years ago, since it happened."

"Why did you quit?" Ren resumed the questioning, leaving Apple to glare distrustfully at Feather.

"Lack of respect in the workplace, mostly. I know it's fast food and all, but I didn't need to be treated so disrespectfully or talked to like I was an imbecile. When a manager is unprofessional and barks at me in front of customers for no apparent reason other than she is having another bad day, I find it is time for me to leave. So, I quit. Other than picking up my final paycheck, I never stepped foot back in the restaurant again. She was not the one on duty when I did return for my money, so the day I vacated my position was the last day I saw her."

"And when did you leave the area?"

"I moved out of Kansas February 25th and came here. I bought this house on March 1st, and I know I had stayed in a hotel as I looked around at the various properties."

"And you didn't return to Kansas any time in March? Not even to get anything you might have left behind?"

"No. I had everything with me when I left in February." Feather really wanted to ask why again, but she knew she wouldn't be told until they had all the answers of whatever they were looking for.

"What about Michael Wesson? Did you know him?"

Feather frowned. "Okay. What's going on?"

"Please, just answer the questions."

"These are pretty obscure questions, Detective Shaw."

"They may seem obscure to you, but they are necessary and I will make the connections shortly. Now please, Feather, please answer the questions."

Feather sighed, her jaw working slightly as she tried to keep calm in order to respond without sounding sarcastic or anything else. The last thing she needed was to get arrested for being obstinate.

"Michael Wesson and I dated a while back for a few months. It wasn't going to go anywhere, but it was fun while it lasted."

"Because he was human or for another reason?"

Feather looked at him astonished he would say that in front of the female detective. Apple must have sensed her concern as she spoke up. "I'm a walker, too."

This gave Feather a chance to breathe a bit more easily. "Yes, Michael was human and, as you know, it can never last with them since we have to keep too many secrets. Besides, he would have figured something out eventually, when he aged and I didn't. Now please, will you tell me what's going on."

"One more. What about Sandra Desmond?"

The name took a moment for Feather to remember. Then she looked up in total shock. "She was the woman I rented the room from just after the Second World War. Raine had just gotten home from the front and we needed a new place to stay. We were only there for a few months before we moved out."

"Are you aware those three, and eleven others that we believe you are familiar with, have since turned up deceased in the same manner as Silver and Paige?"

Feather was stunned. One could knock her over with a strong wind she was so surprised. "Who? Who are the others?"

Apple pulled out the list, moving the coffee to the side. "Let's see. We have John Wellington, Casper Harding, Melody Mitchell, Lisa Evans, Lionel Katz, Penny Harrington, Wilma Washington, Blair Michaels, Victor Embry, Gladys Cooper, and Myles White. According to what we have been able to discover, you knew each and every one of them. True?"

Feather paled as each name was read. Ren watched her closely during the reading and she didn't appear to give off the impression she was guilty or worried that she'd been discovered. She was immensely saddened to learn of the demise of so many people she knew. "All of them? They were all killed like Paige? Like Silver? How can this be?"

Apple stood. "Why don't you tell us down at the station. Feather Woods, you are under arrest for murder."

Even Ren was shocked and stood quickly.

"Why? Because I knew them at one time or other? I didn't know they were dead!" Feather snapped, overwhelmed by the immensity of everything they informed her.

He gave Feather an apologetic look. "Let's go downtown and finish our questioning there. It's going take a while, I venture."

Feather stood. She didn't know what else to do other than to comply. Her mind was totally numb from the entire incident. "I'd never hurt them. Just so you know, I didn't do it. None of it."

They were leading her handcuffed outside when Raine entered the house, having just got home from work. He stopped and growled, blocking their path.

"What the fuck is going on here? Feather? Why is she in cuffs? Where are you taking her?" He directed his questions to Ren, though his eyes kept going over to his partner, who he hadn't seen before. She was unobtrusive, yet that was her appeal. Raine could tell she was a pit bull, someone who looked sweet and weak, but he had the feeling she was a tough cookie when she needed to be.

Sure enough, he was proven correct when she stepped up to him, letting Ren keep a hold on Feather's arm. "I suggest you back up and let us pass. This woman is under arrest and is being removed to our downtown headquarters. She gets a phone call. If she decides to call you, she will let you know what is happening at that point. In the meantime, if you don't get out of the way, I'll arrest you for obstruction of justice."

Raine almost couldn't prevent himself from smiling. He wanted to pat her head like some little Chihuahua who was yapping at his feet. The situation was too serious, however, to give into his imagination or his whim, regardless of how strong the temptation was.

"It's okay, Raine. I'll be okay." Feather was still in shock, her voice betrayed her own disbelief over the names she was read and the fact they were all deceased. She was a shifter, her life long as a result. She was used to people dying, or leaving them behind so they wouldn't notice she was not aging like they were. To find out they were all murdered, and so cruelly, left her feeling unsure of everything around her. She was the link that connected all of them. Not even Raine knew some of the people on the list. Like Michael.

Raine knew his sister well enough to understand that tone in her voice. Something more had happened and she was in shock. He stepped to the side but sent her a mental link to let her know he would get legal assistance and get her free. She would not be spending a night in jail. He realized with her state of mind asking her what recently occurred leading to her arrest would have to wait, as she was still trying to comprehend it herself. Until she did, she wouldn't be able to explain it to him or anyone.

Ren pulled Feather past him and out the door. Apple took hold of Feather's arm and continued to lead her down the stairs and towards the back of the car, but Ren stopped and watched them as he spoke to Raine. "I'll make sure she is treated okay. We really just want to talk to her for a bit. I don't think we will be pressing charges. I'm sure we won't, but we have to do this by the book."

Raine was quiet for a few moments, watching Apple lead Feather away. "I'd appreciate that. I'll be down at the station in a bit to collect her."

"Of course." Without waiting for anything else, Ren bounded down the stairs and got in the driver's seat. Feather peered straight ahead, not even bothering to look out the window at her brother on the top of the stairs watching.

Another telltale sign to Raine something was seriously wrong. His eyes then went over to the female detective. In those couple of moments, she intrigued him. He had never allowed himself to be interested in women before, since his sole goal was to take care of his sister. Yet, the woman partner of Det. Shaw made him reconsider, at least momentarily. It was only when the vehicle was out of sight did he move into the house to take a shower and head downtown to figure out what the hell was going on.

Chapter Twelve

Feather's head was swimming. The more they asked her questions about the people she once knew, and the last time she saw them compared to the dates of their deaths, sent her spiraling down in several unknown directions. She didn't feel like she could breathe, and at times she felt like she was falling. Each one of them were people she had been relatively close to at one point or another. Each one she had left for different reasons, whether it was because they were getting too close to her and therefore her secret, or because they had verbal disagreements, or as a result of a variety of other obscure reasons. Regardless, within days, and in some cases hours, after she told them good-bye, they were tortured and killed.

Ren was more convinced than ever that she was innocent. No one was that good of an actress, especially to a shifter who was exceptionally adept at ferreting out lies. Even Apple had to give in to the fact Feather didn't seem to know what had happened to any of them and had she, herself, not found Paige, she would never have been aware of the tormented states their bodies were discovered.

"Let's go through it one more time." Apple sat across from Feather, a folder open with all of the pictures of the previous deceased put together. Before and after pictures. Ren had enough. He felt like he was torturing Feather and he just couldn't do it. He was also given notification Raine had arrived at the station and was asking for them.

Quietly, Ren stepped out and headed to the lobby to meet Raine, bringing him back to his desk. He held his hand out for the chair alongside of it, indicating for Raine to sit. Raine plopped down and crossed one leg over his knee. Ren noticed he was looking around. "Feather is in interrogation. She had refused a lawyer, but we're still getting a few answers."

"You do realize whatever you are accusing her of, she is innocent."

"Yes. I'm aware. I believe Detective Shade is also, but we need to find out a few things. She is more of a person of interest with some answers, at the moment, than under arrest. I'm sorry Feather was removed so dramatically from your home. Shade can be a bit single-minded in certain things." He had no idea why he was telling Raine all of this, but he couldn't help it. Maybe it was to make him realize he wouldn't do anything to harm her, despite the fact she was not his to protect, but Raine's.

"Detective Shade? That's your female partner?"

"Yes. Sorry. I guess there wasn't time for introductions."

Raine looked around, then sighed. *Best to bite the bullet.* "Is she…your partner? I mean. Is she available?"

Ren quirked an eyebrow. "She is not mated or dating or anything. Why?"

"Just curious." Raine looked around the room. "She likes guys though, right?"

"Yeah. She does." Ren frowned, almost glaring at Raine. "Look, I know you care about Feather. Just don't be cruel to her. She loves you so much."

"I know Feather does. I feel the same way about her."

"Feather is going through a lot of things right now. She needs you to be faithful to her. She needs your protection."

"I'll always protect Feather. She's my responsibility. Why are you telling me this?"

Ren thought a moment. "Would you protect her enough to do anything to keep her for yourself?" The police in him wondered if he'd kill to keep her to himself. In his line of work, he was very aware of how possessive some men could be, even to the point of murder. If they can't be his, they wouldn't be anyone's kind of thought process. Gods, Feather was so beautiful, so sweet and loving. He desperately wished he was the one she cared about. How lucky to be the man she loved. But she was someone else's. She was Raine's and he wouldn't interfere. He respected her to accept her choice. However, someone didn't respect it. Someone didn't respect her. Someone wanted her all to themself. Someone possessive, who would see her cut off from the rest of the world. Someone, maybe, like Raine. Yet, Raine was also willing to cheat on her? Could a person be so possessive that they would kill to keep a woman to themselves and still desire another?

"For myself? What kind of fucking bullshit are you talking about?" Raine was totally lost. Did the man think because he cared for Feather, he couldn't have a woman of his own? A future? A family? He had just never met anyone who caught his interest before, not like Shaw's partner.

"I have seen how you look at Det. Shade, and now you are asking questions about her. I don't want Feather hurt because of it."

Raine gave him a puzzled look. "How I look at your partner has nothing to do with her or with you."

Ren growled low and leaned over towards Raine. "You son of a bitch. You are so goddamned lucky to have someone as beautiful and loyal as Feather! How could you even think of cheating on her?"

"Cheating? What the fuck, dude? I love her and protect her 'cause she's my sister, not my mate."

Ren was startled, and that wasn't something he could say lightly. In his line of work, it was rare things could surprise him. Mortify him, astound him, make him wonder where the heads of humanity lie, but surprise him? Not so much. Yet, Raine managed just that, and at the same time gave him a sense of hope he hadn't felt in ages. "Your sister?"

Realization dawned on Raine. The detective was sweet on Feather and thought they were a couple. He smiled. "Yeah. My baby sister, to be exact. Ever since our mother died, I have cared for her. Our father was a drunken, abusive asshole and I was the only one she could rely on. She's my sister, dude. I'll always love and protect her, but not in the way you were thinking."

Ren scrubbed his face as he sat back. "I must seem like the most foolish detective on the face of the planet, that I couldn't even figure out you two were siblings and not mates. Sorry, man."

Raine sat up, slapping Ren's shoulder lightly. "Look. I've watched how you've been trying to protect her and make sure she is safe, as well as handle the shit that's going on around her."

Ren interjected. "Dude, you have no idea. She is involved in a lot more than just Silver and Paige."

This made Raine's eyebrows shoot up. "More?"

"Yes. I probably shouldn't be telling you this, but I am beginning to see a pattern here I'm just not very comfortable with. There has been a total of sixteen deaths we can attribute, irrefutably, to the same perp, and each one of the victims knew Feather in one way or another."

"If they knew her, then they knew me. Maybe I can help? What kind of pattern are you thinking about?"

"Actually, yeah. Maybe you can help. Follow me." Ren stood and motioned Raine to follow him to an interrogation room. He then left him alone for a few minutes as he went next door to talk to Apple and let him know he was going to question Raine, who volunteered to talk to them. He also let her know he had an idea and to turn the questioning towards potential mates for Feather that she might've been aware of. Creatures who would want her but couldn't have her, whether for lack of interest or something else. Someone who might have a grudge against her or want her all to themselves, essentially cutting her off from everyone else. Apple nodded in understanding to his whispered instructions and turned back to Feather, pulling out a clean sheet of paper for all the notes she would make.

"Let's start over and from the beginning." Apple licked the tip of the pencil and hovered it over the paper.

When Ren walked into the room where Raine was waiting, he sat down opposite him with a notepad and a folder containing the list of names of those who matched the MO of the killer.

One by one they went through the names, the dates of the murders, where he and Feather were at during the hours the crimes were committed, and if they were even aware these people had been killed. The answers were pretty much the same as Feather had given to the detectives earlier.

Raine scrubbed his face and held his head in his hands. "I can't believe all of these people! I can't believe we never knew."

"Is there something in particular that happened in 1948?"

"How do you mean?"

"Well, something changed for this guy. We can't find anyone who fits the profile for his kind of operation prior to that time. So, what set him off? What changed?"

Raine sat back, grabbing the coffee Ren had brought in about an hour back. It was cold, but he didn't care. It was wet and it gave him something to do with his hands while he tried to think back almost seventy years. "The war had been over for a couple of years, but I only got home the year prior. As a code talker, we had a lot of communiqués that had to be translated, then put in the codes after the war from the surrendered countries. That took almost two years, once the war was officially over. We, Feather and I, knew we needed to move soon. We had been in Oklahoma a bit too long at that point and moved into El Paso in '48. I remember Feather hated to leave. She was comfortable there and sure we could've had a few more years before we attracted suspicion from the locals. Honestly, we probably could have, but I wanted something different after the war. I was antsy. I wanted someplace more quiet than the big cities there. I'd had my full of them in Europe and just wanted—needed—quiet. I had to stop hearing the big guns constantly going off."

Ren nodded. "I understand. Although I didn't serve in the big one, I was in Vietnam. It's tough when you first get back. Every backfiring car sets your teeth on edge, every yell makes your skin crawl, and you keep waiting for a grenade to land at your feet or to step on a landmine. It's nerve wracking."

"Why did you go into police work, then?"

Ren sat back and folded his hands on his belly.

He thought about it for a moment before he answered. "I guess, I felt it was someplace I fit. I was going to be jumpy anyways, my senses were on high alert, so why not put it to good use? Besides, I have this innate need to help others and make sure they stay safe. It's why I joined the Marines to begin with. Besides, I can remain here for a good number of years, since a lot of the upper echelon are our kind. Plus with all the stuff they have now, we just tell the humans we are undergoing plastic surgery or something and get a few more years out of it."

"That's cool. The world has changed. We get lost in it sometimes. It's good to know there is some stable structure than can be counted on."

"Her name is Apple, by the way."

"Excuse me?"

"Apple Shade. My partner. Her name is Apple. She hates it, though."

Raine smiled. "Thanks. You think she will give me a shot if I don't call her Apple? At least to start?" Gods, his mind went through all sorts of things at her name. She is the apple of his eye. A little rain will make the apple grow. An apple a day keeps the gloom away. Yeah, he could see why she would hate her name, as his mind continued with more clichéd sayings.

"I honestly don't know her type, so I can't really say. She never talks about guys with me other than the general stuff." Ren sat up, a serious look on his face. "What about Feather? I know this is a perfectly shitty ass time, but, do you think she would be interested?"

Raine shrugged. "My sister is complicated. I can't really say. I sometimes think she has a heart too huge to contain. She believes the best in everyone and in everything. I can't imagine she wouldn't give you a chance, beyond that though? No fucking clue."

"Fair enough."

"I would suggest you wait a day or so before you ask her out. Asking her the same day as you arrest her and question her about all this stuff is not entirely conducive to asking her out and getting a yes. But, if you do ask her and she agrees, you better treat her like a queen. Her favorite flowers are white calla lilies and pink roses. She likes dark chocolate and it's better if it has caramel that's gooey and she likes ice cream. She is fairly simple in what she does, so nothing uber fancy." Raine figured if he gave him some tidbits about Feather, Ren would reciprocate and tell him more about Apple.

"What about boyfriends or suitors? Did she reject any?"

"Now?" Raine was lost.

"Sorry. No. In '48. Were there any particularly interested suitors that you're aware of, which she might have rejected?"

"Oh. Time warp." Raine thought about it for a few moments, then shook his head no. "Not that I am aware of. Before the war, I would say yes, but after, no. She pretty much kept to herself."

"What about the one before the war?"

Raine shook his head. "Payne River. He was like a brother to us, and though he asked me for permission to mate her, I never broached the subject with her. We were being shipped out a couple of weeks later. Feather got notice he was killed at the Battle of the Bulge."

"So much for that idea." Ren sighed. "Apple likes daisies and sunflowers. She says they are happy flowers and no one can't help but smile when they see them. She is also a huge taco eater. Loves Casa Rio. Makes me eat there at least once a week, more if I let her. And she finds the Paseo de Rio boat cruise romantic if done at night. Come on. Let's go get the girls and you can take Feather home. I'm sure she is exhausted by now since we have had her most of the day."

Another hour later, papers were signed and Feather was released to Raine. He nodded to Ren and smiled at Apple, thanking them both as he escorted a very weary and distraught Feather back home.

Chapter Thirteen

He stood watching as they left the police station, hidden by the rich foliage of the trees. They were to blame for everything. They would pay. He had made those he thought were close to them pay, but they were barely aware. Now, now was the time he went after both of them for what they did to him. She should be his. He should have allowed it. Instead, he suffered by their inconsiderate behavior, by their neglect. No. They would pay. And the time was at hand.

So many had gotten in the way. He lived to kill, to absorb the souls of others, then watch them die at his hand. The thought of it made him hard. Especially when he remembered his latest conquest, Silver. She hadn't been on his list originally, but she'd found out about him and he couldn't risk her talking to Feather or anyone else. He could remember each of those whose hearts he feasted upon, whose eyes hung in the pouch at his waist. He could remember every thought they had in life, from the moment they were born to the moment he stripped them of their very souls and made them immortal through him.

He wondered what the police spoke to them about. Feather had been arrested, brought into the station in handcuffs by the female detective. She would be the first to pay. Then the male. Neither would be let off for treating Feather as they had. Then, it would be time to get Raine out of the picture. Again, the thought of it being his fault entered his mind. Yes, Raine would pay, and then Feather. She would either be his or she would live on in him as did the others. There was no other thought as important to him as the last one. He had things to get ready, steps to take. First would be the female cop.

* * *

Raine couldn't get Apple out of his mind, even though he desperately wanted to. He didn't have time for relationships, and he sure as hell didn't need to be in one. Yet, she was so feisty, and spirited in just those few moments he met her at the house, and then later at the police station. Every word she spoke reverberated within his mind repeatedly. He found himself smiling at just the thought of her. What the fuck was wrong with him? He was never like this before, never considered a woman to be anything other than a dalliance at best. Yet, here he was, unable to get the little spitfire out of his mind.

He couldn't stand it anymore. He needed to do something about this sudden obsession he had with her. Raine realized he had one of two choices: he could either seek her out, or he could go to a strip club and let others wipe out whatever the fuck stuck with him about her. A couple of lap dances, some singles down a couple of g-strings? Yes. It would all be better.

He chose the latter and got into his blue Dodge Ram truck and headed for the nearest gentlemen's club, The Foxy Trot. The parking lot was already three-quarters full when he pulled up. Putting the truck in park, he rubbed his face. What the fuck was he doing? Oh yeah, getting Apple Shade out of his mind.

He climbed out of the truck and headed towards the door, but stopped when he heard a whistle. As he turned, he couldn't believe it. *What the fuck was she doing here?* Raine turned to face Det. Shade as she approached, crossing his arms across his chest.

"Following me now?" he growled out harshly. How was he supposed to get her out of his mind if he kept running into her?

"Don't flatter yourself. You're just about to get in the way and I'd prefer to keep all innocents from being part of a major smuggling ring. Why are you here, anyways?" She had moved close to him, so her words wouldn't be overheard. She took his arm and led him back to his truck as if that was what they'd planned all along. She literally shoved him into his cab and slammed the door. Behind her, the world broke loose. Squad cars, their lights blazing, pulled up and surrounded the building. Uniformed police rushed the building, weapons drawn.

"Get out of here!" she ordered, then turned, pulled her sweater off to show the police vest underneath, pulled her weapon out and dashed to the entryway of the club.

Raine sat in the cab, afraid to move. Leave it to him to pick the place that was being raided by the woman who he was trying desperately to get out of his mind. He watched the action go down, not totally out of morbid curiosity, but also out of concern. Of course, that he was blocked in by the other police cars didn't help his escape either.

He stepped out of the cab to watch, but stayed close to his truck and out of the way of the busy civil servants. Minutes ticked by while he waited. She didn't have to go to him. She could've let him venture inside and deal with the consequences of whatever was going down in there. Smuggling. He wondered what they were smuggling. Money? Drugs? Girls? Guns? Shit. All he wanted to do was have a few mindless minutes without thinking of one female who sparked the blood in his veins.

What seemed like hours later, several police officers in their vests came out, leading several men to a waiting police van. If a couple more cars moved along with the van, he'd be able to get his truck out and leave the scene, too. A bar and some good, old-fashioned alcohol might do the trick since this was an entire epic fail.

His feline hearing allowed him to discern a stockpile of weapons were recovered. Some of them were believed to be used in previous homicides and would have to undergo ballistic tests to determine if they matched any open cases. His feline sight picked up Apple as soon as she came out of the building, holding the bicep of a rather formidable-looking man.

Once they were outside, the man elbowed her in the face before he took off running. Straight for Raine. Great. He was going to get shot while just standing there as an observer. Raine braced himself, ready to tackle the escaped man, but he never got the chance to engage him. Det. Shade pounced on him from behind, knocking him to his knees. She quickly got up and moved in front of him, standing between Raine and the man. When the guy stood, he was ready to slug Apple, but she ducked and hit him in the gut. Backing up, she swiveled and kicked him so he was back down again. Two other uniformed police officers rushed to her side, arriving just as the man fell. Each one grabbed an arm and pulled it back, slapping cuffs on him. Why they weren't on him to begin with, he couldn't fathom, but it wasn't his call on procedure.

Regardless, he was thoroughly impressed with the little vixen he was beginning to think of as his.

"I thought I told you to get out of here." She wiped the blood off her split lip from when she was elbowed in the face.

"Kinda blocked in. Had no choice but to stay and watch the show."

"This ain't funny. Get out of here."

"I will, *if* you'll have dinner with me."

Apple's mouth dropped open. "Are you asking me on a date?"

"I guess I am."

"This is highly inappropriate."

"So? It's more interesting this way. I also noticed you didn't say no."

"I didn't say yes, either."

"But, you didn't say no. I'll pick you up at 7:30 tomorrow."

"No. You can pick me up at eight on Friday. I have too much work to do in the meantime."

"Eight on Friday it is. I need your address, though."

"I have your info from the case. I'll text it to you tomorrow."

"If you don't, I'll sit on the precinct steps until you show up."

"You are persistent."

"It's one of my better qualities."

Apple snorted. "Get out of here. I can't concentrate on my job with you hanging about and worrying about your civilian ass."

"Yes, Ms. Bad Ass." Raine spun on his heel and got into his truck. After several attempts, he was finally able to get out of the parking lot and head home.

* * *

Several days had gone by since Raine made the date with Apple. Her name still made him smile, but the jokes that had abounded within his head slowly subsided. He had finally asked her out and she, surprisingly, accepted. He was getting ready, grateful for the heads up from Shaw on what she liked. He planned a whole evening. Dinner at her favorite restaurant, followed by an intimate cruise on the river afterwards. He rented out a whole boat so it would just be the two of them. It cost a pretty penny to do that, but he didn't care. First impressions were the most important. He couldn't remember being this excited over a date in his entire life.

A knock on his door broke his reverie and he called for Feather to come in.

"Hey, bro. So, tonight is the big night?"

"Yes. Just getting ready now. What do you think?" He looked down at himself while she appraised him.

"Your collar is messed up. Here." She moved over and fixed his collar, then tapped his shoulders. "It's nice to see you this excited about seeing someone."

"I feel odd. Like I'm abandoning you or something."

"Don't, Raine. You deserve this. You have looked after me for eons. This time is yours. Enjoy it. Don't worry about me."

"What are you going to do while I'm out?"

"Detective Shaw asked if he could come over. I thought it would be alright. Besides, he wanted to be sure I wasn't alone, considering everything going on. I figured you put him up to it, so you wouldn't feel guilty for leaving me. You know, I'm not sure if I mentioned this or not, but I met him before."

"What do you mean before? Before what?"

"Before all this happened. He was the one who met the group of us at the train station before taking us to Xulth to be educated in our gifts."

Raine frowned. "No. I was unaware of this." He grabbed his sibling's shoulders, holding her still to peer into her amber eyes as if seeking answers within the openings to her soul. When he was satisfied, he let her go. "You liked him then. You like him now."

Feather could have denied it, but why? She had always been honest, especially to her brother, and she was not about to change that now. "Yeah. I do. He was kind to me that first night at the camp. I was scared and nervous and he helped to calm me. He has been kind recently, as well. His partner was the one who wanted to bring me downtown for questions. He made sure I was comfortable and gave me the benefit of the doubt, which aided in my release. He is sympathetic to everything that is going on with Paige and Silver, and the others before them. He seems to understand how upset I am and isn't judgmental, and I appreciate that."

"He likes you, you know."

She snorted in derision. "How would you

know?"

"He told me." He turned to check himself in the mirror once again. "He thought we were mates, and when I showed interest in his partner, I think he was ready to shoot me for being unfaithful to you." He watched her in the mirror for her reaction. He was gratified to see her smile at the thought, then give a soft chuckle.

"He thought we were mates? I'm not sure whether to be insulted or not."

"You couldn't ever get someone as wonderful as me for a mate. No matter how hard you try."

She moved up behind him, resting her head on his shoulder, her arm around the back of his waist. "You're right. I'll have to settle for second best to you. You're the best brother anyone could ever have and I don't think I've told you how much I appreciate you."

Raine turned around and pulled her into a tight hug, holding her close against his body. "You never have to tell me that. You're my sister. I love you and I'll always be here when you need me. I've never regretted having you as a sibling. If anything, you gave me purpose, especially in my youth. I'd have given up a hundred times over when Father... Well, I would've given up, but I needed to fight for life to be with you. To protect you as I promised I would. I couldn't have asked for a better sibling."

She continued to hug him a bit more, then took a step back. His words made her very emotional and she couldn't speak. She gave him one more look, then nodded. "You're going to be late. Don't keep the girl waiting."

Raine looked at the time. "Shit. Gotta go." He kissed her cheek and dashed out the bedroom. Grabbing his jacket, he flung open the front door just as Ren was about to ring the doorbell. "Go on in," he called to him as he dashed past and jumped in his truck.

Ren followed him with his eyes for a moment, then turned to see Feather standing at the open entryway watching him. "I should give him a ticket for speeding," he teased, then held out a bouquet of white roses and calla lilies. "For you," he added nervously.

She took the flowers, a smile spreading across her face. "Thank you. Come in?"

Ren entered and she shut the door behind him. "I'm going to put these in a vase. Pour yourself a drink. If I don't have what you want there, I probably do in one of the cabinets underneath." She called back to him as she entered the kitchen. He went over to the bar and poured himself a club soda. He was never much of a drinker. He didn't like the way it clouded his thoughts. He hoped she wasn't, either, but it was a concern considering the array of alcoholic choices at the side bar.

"Can I pour you something?" he called to her in the other room.

"Club soda, please, and a squeeze of lime."

Ren smiled as he fixed her drink. Maybe it was Raine who was the drinker. Considering they both had told him their father was an abusive alcoholic, he was rather surprised if one of them was as well. But then, maybe the fruit didn't fall far from the tree. Since Feather asked for club soda, Raine must be the one who drank. Suddenly he was concerned that Raine might also be abusive. She could be under a type of Stockholm Syndrome, staying by her sibling's side regardless of duress. Their relationship was certainly close.

Sometimes being a cop was not the best thing as he thought the worst of most people. It was a mentality that kept him on his toes and allowed him to survive so much. It was also what allowed him to be a good detective, permitting him to see past the lies of the criminals to the truth. At least until now. Raine and Feather completely flummoxed him. Every time he thought one thing about them, he was totally incorrect. He hoped his current thoughts also proved erroneous. He would hate to have Feather abused by her brother the way she was by their father.

It had been one of the many things they had talked about during that night so long ago, but he had never forgotten their conversations. Except that she had a brother. Had she told him? She must have and he had suppressed the information.

His musings were broken when she returned to put the vase of flowers he gave her on the buffet nearby. Whiskers jumped up to sniff them; Feather shooed the cat off the buffet. Ren moved over to her, handing her the club soda with lime she asked for. "That's quite an extensive bar you have. I'm surprised with all there was to choose from you only wanted a club soda." He thought if he were subtle, he might find out the truth of the matter without seeming like he was prying.

She waved her hand dismissively. "Neither Raine nor I drink, but we keep it around in case any of our guests do. Though, ironically, we don't have many guests, either."

He was rather grateful to ascertain neither were alcoholics and his original belief that Raine protected her was correct. He joined her on the couch, his own soda in hand. Whiskers jumped on Feather's lap, albeit her eyes were on Ren as she settled on Feather.

"Thank you for coming over tonight."

"My pleasure."

"I think Raine preferred I wasn't alone tonight, considering everything going on."

"I know it makes me feel better that you're not left unprotected. Your brother seems to really take care of you and is concerned."

"He does. He always has. Ever since we were kids."

"He told me about your father, being abusive and an alcoholic."

Feather nodded. "Growing up, Raine took the brunt of punishments from him and did the most to make sure I was unharmed and safe. He took the role of parent most of the time. I missed him so much when I was sent to the mountains. I really cannot stress to you enough how grateful I am that you stayed with me. I know now how inappropriate that was to ask of you and you were a perfect gentleman the whole time. You could've done anything to me. I was so naïve."

"I'm not that kind of person to take advantage towards anyone like that. It's not how I was raised or who I am."

"You were lucky."

"I was. I am. My family consists of six brothers and five sisters. My parents are loving and respectful. They've had hard times with the cultural changes, but we stick together and see the others through it. Like you and Raine do. We lean on each other, support and help however we can."

"Do they all live in San Antonio?"

"No. Over the years they spread out. Nebraska, Louisiana, Oklahoma, Kansas and Missouri, as well as other cities in Texas: El Paso, Ft. Worth and Austin."

"Do you miss them?"

"I miss the closeness of a big family. I don't miss being underfoot all the time." He chuckled. "I'd like to build a large family of my own one day. With the right person, of course." Ren's eyes never left Feather's. To him, she was the right person, but he didn't want to spook her with his feelings. He was fully aware she needed to get to know him better, and that they both needed to earn each other's trust. Her brother was all she'd ever had to protect and guide her. He knew she'd need time to adjust to the possibility of another taking his place. "Raine seems to really like Shade."

Feather gave an almost sad smile and looked down at Whiskers as she rubbed her fur. "It's the first time I've ever seen him so excited by someone. I'm glad. He deserves to find happiness."

"You make it sound like you don't."

She chuckled softly. "No. We all do. I just don't think I'm going to find it so easily."

"Why?"

She shrugged. "Men make me nervous. I'm not comfortable with them."

"You seem to be okay with me."

She grinned. "I guess I am. You're easy to talk to and I still remember that night so long ago. Your kindness and sweetness."

Ren was quiet a moment. His head screamed at him to just tell her how he felt. Why was he being such a wimp about it? For shit's sake, he was ex-military, fought in Vietnam, was a street cop who worked his way up to one of the top detectives on the force. And he was a complete monkey turd for not having the guts to tell her how he felt. *Suck it up, buttercup*, he admonished himself. "I'm grateful you find me easy to converse with." *Say it.* "Truth is, I like you. From the moment I saw you get off that train, I found you captivating. I should never have checked on you or the others once we got to the camp, but I hated the idea of not seeing you or talking to you some more. I wanted to get to know you better. I needed to understand why I suddenly felt different than I'd ever felt before with you near." Ren let his eyes drift to Whiskers, glad he could look elsewhere and not meet her possibly judgmental eyes. "When I realized who you were at Paige's, I thought I was being given a second chance to be with you."

Feather's hand stopped petting Whiskers as she thought about everything he disclosed to her. Then she thought about how she was feeling before she felt confident enough to say anything in return. "I'm very appreciative of you telling me all this." She reached out her hand and touched his lightly.

"Maybe the fates or gods or whatever made sure our paths crossed again. Maybe a part of me always knew of your interest. I only know the truth of what I feel. You've made me feel comfortable. I've never been afraid to be alone with you, or concerned for my safety in any respect. That sounds silly, I guess, but considering the men who've gotten close, Raine was the only other I've ever been relaxed to be around, except for you. I think I like you, too. I know I'd like to get to know you better. Maybe there can be more between us."

She started to pull her hand away, but he snatched it back into his own, bringing it up to his lips. "I'd like that as well."

Chapter Fourteen

Apple sat next to Raine as he drove the truck towards the river. He had brought her sunflowers, which she had on her lap, as they drove through the city. As soon as he pulled into the Casa Rio parking lot, she couldn't help but give him a raised eyebrow. "Who have you been talking to?"

"Excuse me?"

"My favorite flowers, my favorite restaurant. I'm not stupid. You had to talk to someone or you are a stalker. Which is it?"

Raine barked out a laugh. "I'm not a stalker. I'm a good detective," he teased lightly.

Now it was her turn to laugh. "I'll keep that in mind." She had a feeling he talked to her partner, but since he wouldn't admit it, she really had no proof to the matter.

Raine parked the truck and took the ticket. He offered his arm to her as they walked down the ramp to river level for a table. The sun was just starting to set as the hostess led them to a seat along the Paseo de Rio. She had to smile as she looked out over the water, the boats going past and the drivers narrating the various locations as they passed. Even a greenish-gray police boat drove by, the driver nodding to those seated along the water.

The colorful umbrellas were lit with twinkling little lights, making them stand out in the darkening sky. Although she didn't need to look at the menu, knowing it by heart, Raine didn't have that advantage. After a few moments, he set the menu aside. "I've a feeling you know exactly what is good here, so I will have the same as you do."

Apple smiled. "I'm partial to the tacos. I like getting the three plate, but sometimes I like to mix it up with the choose-two choices and get the tacos and an enchilada. Honestly, everything is good here."

"I like the combination plate. Enchiladas and tacos sound excellent. Did you want a margarita? It looks like they are famous here for that as well."

"They are, but I'm good with water."

Raine's smile widened. As a result of his

father's drinking, he preferred not to be around those who liked to drink. At best, Feather and he were occasional social drinkers, but preferred water or club soda to anything else. A momentary thought wondered how she was doing with Ren, but his focus quickly returned to the stunning woman across the table from him.

Throughout dinner, Raine and Apple talked, telling each other a bit about their past, growing up in the reservations, dealing with the boarding schools and more. Time flew and Raine couldn't have been happier if he tried. Except, he kept feeling as if they were being watched. It was an eerie feeling, and though the Riverwalk was crowded as always, it was not unusually so. He was sure it was just his imagination to have the feeling of being observed, but no matter how hard he tried to shake the feeling, he just couldn't. So he ignored it as best he could, which wasn't too difficult considering he was entranced with his female company. Still, that little nagging feeling kept him on alert. He wasn't going to take any chances she might be hurt or something was going to happen. Not on his watch. He didn't care if she was a detective and could probably kick his ass if she wanted to. He had always been in the role of protector and he knew nothing else.

Too soon for his liking, dinner was completed. He excused himself to make a quick phone call, then returned to her, leading Apple to the river gate of the restaurant. Within moments, a barge pulled up and opened the gate. Apple looked at him, surprised. "Shall we?" Raine gestured.

She shook her head in amazement, but climbed in and took a seat. Raine moved to sit next to her, putting his arm around her. As soon as they were both seated, they took off. Since Ren had told him Apple did this often, he made sure the captain didn't bother with narration. The quietness of the night on the water was enough for him. They made small talk.

"Have you been on the river barges before?" Apple snuggled against him.

"Not really. Seemed a bit touristy to me."

Raine wrapped his arm around her, grateful she wasn't shy with him.

"They are, but there is something about them, about being on the water and letting the world pass. It's just rejuvenating. At least to me."

"I can understand that much better now that I'm on one. I'm glad my first time is with you."

She smiled at him, leaning back against him and pointing out some of the things the driver would have if this were a full tour instead of a private charter. "That's a statue of St. Anthony. Over there is La Villita. They have some wonderful shops there. Lots of artistic things."

Raine listened and looked whenever she pointed something out. He knew most of the buildings, but had to admit, from the water they looked slightly different. All the lit-up buildings made them stand out even more.

Apple wondered if he was really listening to her ramble on, or even if he cared to know the inane things she was telling him. She turned to face him, to ask if she should be quiet and just let him enjoy the ride. She never had a chance. As soon as she turned to ask, his lips were on hers.

Raine stunned himself with his audacity. He hadn't planned on kissing her, but as soon as she faced him, he was overcome with the desire to know what she tasted like. Tacos and honey. The latter probably from the sopapillas they had for dessert, small puffed pillows of pastry covered with cinnamon and honey. It was the first time he had them and they were delicious. He pulled back almost immediately. "Sorry. I just couldn't resist."

Apple didn't say anything. Instead, she grabbed the back of his head and pulled him back to her, letting their lips touch once again. She was the aggressor. It was her tongue that pushed against his lips, wanting entrance, and he willingly gave it.

They spent the rest of the hour-long ride kissing. She had no idea where they were or what they passed. All she knew was the ride was over way too quickly. The captain coughed a couple of times to get their attention, then had to blatantly announce they were back. Raine reluctantly pulled back, kissing the tip of her nose as he did so. "Come on." He took her hand and helped her back onto the Riverwalk. He gave the captain a hundred-dollar tip and led Apple back to his truck.

As he closed the passenger door with her inside, he stopped and looked around. The feeling of being watched was overpowering. He used his feline senses to determine where it was coming from, who might be watching them, but they were in a very populated city and it was more difficult to narrow down. At least in the country it was easy to hone in on the location of whatever or whoever it might be.

It reminded him of Payne watching him at the base of the Guadalupe Mountains, only Payne was dead and the city was too populated to figure out where he was being watched from. Raine gave another look around, then climbed into the cab of the truck before driving Apple back to her place.

He walked her to her door and kissed her goodnight. "Thank you for going out with me. I hope you will accompany me again soon."

"I'd like that very much. It's been a very long time since I have had this much fun or enjoyed myself so much. Thank you."

He kissed her cheek, leaning over her. "It was my pleasure." Turning, he headed back to his truck, but stopped, looking around once again. Still not seeing anything unusual, he got in and drove away after making sure she got inside safely.

When she turned on her lights, she looked out the window and saw Raine pull away. A smile was still on her lips at the thought of the night and the kisses as she pulled the drapes closed. When she turned around, she was not alone.

Her training kicked in. She reached for her gun tucked into her side holster hidden by her jacket. Pulling it out quickly, she aimed it at the unknown subject trespassing in her home.

"Hands up. You picked the wrong house, asshole."

"Apple Shade. Did you have a good time tonight? Did you have fun with Raine Woods? Kissing him? Did you want to make love to him?

Have his body pressed against yours?"

"Why? You got a crush on him or something? Sorry, but I don't think he would be interested. You can try, though, but just saying. Now get your hands up or the next thing will be my pistol doing all the talking." She wondered how he got in or how he knew her name. Was she being stalked?

With the speed of a preternatural being, he was beside her, knocking the gun out of her hand. Apple Shade was a trained police officer, though. Sure, she dropped the pistol to the floor and he still had a good hold of her wrist in the process, but she was small enough to twist under his arm, bring it around slightly and, using her stance, hip, and his weight, flip him onto the floor.

Where some self-defense classes taught to watch the eyes of the attacker to anticipate what move would come next, she found the twist of shoulders more telltale. Her attacker seemed stunned. Then it dawned on her. He didn't realize she was a shifter as well. She was paler than most Native Americans due to breeding outside of her gifted tribe. She rarely discussed her parentage with anyone, so it wasn't obvious she was one of the favored. Her background was unnecessary for the career or life path she chose to follow in becoming a police officer.

He was shocked when she flipped him. He only needed a moment for her to look into his eyes, but she seemed to be avoiding them. He scrambled to his feet while letting his fingernails elongate into talons. He slashed at her. Her own reflexes allowed her to jump back, but not far enough as he caught her shoulder, tearing her blouse, her blood staining it.

She rolled away from him and towards her fallen weapon in order to retrieve it. As she came up, he backhanded her. Apple fell against the table, but she held onto the pistol. She shot wildly towards his direction. He dove through the window, glass breaking, and ran before he shifted and disappeared into the darkened night. She ran to the window and peered out, trying to find him.

Pulling her phone out with one hand as she

clutched the gun with the other in case he tried to return, she speed dialed her partner. She took another look out the window, then moved to a chair, feeling a bit dizzy from the blood loss. He clawed her deeper than she originally thought, a burning pain was slowly spreading across the wounds he inflicted upon her. Her adrenaline was subsiding and the resulting injury was beginning to take precedence on her attention.

"Hello?" Ren answered the phone. He knew from the caller ID it was Apple, but she was supposed to be on a date with Raine and he couldn't imagine why she would be calling.

"Ren. Fucker was here. Need help."

He could hear her labored breathing and he stood quickly. "Your place?"

She grunted a yes in response.

"On my way. Hold on, Shade. You hear me? You better fucking hold on." Ren disconnected the call, giving an apologetic look to Feather. "Something's wrong. I'm sorry. I gotta go."

Feather followed him to the door, concern

clearly etched on her features. He pulled the door open only to see Raine about to enter the house. Raine immediately knew something was wrong when Ren growled, grabbed his collar and shoved him against the side of the house.

Raine tried to shake him off. "What the fuck are you doing? What's going on?"

"Shade. Something happened. What the fuck did you do to her?" Ren snarled, his concern on getting to her quickly overwhelmed by the need to beat Raine's ass to a pulp for whatever he did.

Raine shoved him back. "I didn't do anything. What do you mean something happened?" Unlike Ren, his concern was for Apple and he wasn't about to waste any unnecessary time in getting to her. "You can explain on the way or stay the fuck here, I don't give a damn, but I'm going to make sure she is okay." He jumped down the five stairs and ran to his truck, hopping in.

Ren hesitated for a moment, stupefied. Feather, however, didn't waste any more time. She grabbed her keys off the rack by the door, slammed it shut and pulled Ren towards the truck, shoving him in next to her brother. "Go!" she commanded once she slammed the cab's door closed.

Raine broke a million speed laws getting back to Apple's place. He had no idea how bad it was, or even what happened, and the fact that Ren didn't know either but was concerned just made him wig out even more. If anything happened to her, Raine wouldn't be able to deal with it. He knew it. What could've happened? He had just left her not twenty minutes ago. She got into the house safely. He made sure of that. She waved to him from the window before he drove off. So, what the fuck happened in the meantime?

He pulled alongside the curb in front of her place, not caring that he was also on the lawn, slightly diagonal from the street. He ran towards the door, Feather and Ren on his heels. Raine tested the knob, but the door was locked. He was about to kick it down, but Ren stopped him, grabbing a spare key from a ledge above the door. Waving it in front of Raine's face to get him to not kick him while he unlocked it, they all dashed in, calling and looking for her.

"Shade?" Raine ran straight to where he last saw her by the window and found her slumped in a chair. "In here. Feather, call 911."

Ren rushed to the other side of her, grabbing her wrist to check for a pulse. "She's still alive, but has lost a lot of blood. Shade? Come on, partner. Can you hear me? I'm here."

"We're here. Don't you give up on me, Apple. Come on, baby. Wake up."

She didn't stir. Not at first. Raine looked back as Feather disconnected her call. "They're on their way. I told them she was a police officer. On TV, cops seem to get faster service, so I thought it might help."

"Good thinking. Thank you." Ren nodded, turning back to his partner. He looked around the room. Overturned chairs, broken glass, and knocked over items indicated there was a struggle. He needed her awake in order to know the details. The wounds looked like deep claw marks across her chest, the blood pooling on the floor in maroon droplets.

Raine pulled his own shirt off and used it to try and stop the flow. His free hand brushed back the hair from her forehead as he cooed to her to wake up and that she would be alright. "Help is on the way. Come on, Apple. Wake up."

Feather felt useless as the two men hovered near Apple. Ren got on the phone and called the department, bringing them up to date on what occurred thus far. He also indicated he needed a forensics team. "Yes. I'll keep you up to date on her condition, sir. There was definitely a struggle and we have disturbed some evidence by mistake as a result. I'll file a report when I leave the hospital, but I'm not leaving my partner until I know she is safe. Yes, sir. Will do." He pressed the end-call button and turned to Raine. "We're going to need to get your prints on file. We already have Feather's from a few days ago, but we'll need yours to eliminate those around here."

"Whatever you need to catch the son of a bitch

that did this," Raine growled. Feather laid her hand on his shoulder for silent support, but looked up as she heard sirens.

"I'll go let them in." It gave Feather an excuse to feel useful, having felt anything but since they arrived.

One paramedic dashed in and followed Feather to where Apple was. Both men moved out of the way to give the emergency techs room to maneuver, but both stayed close, as well. Moments later, two more came in pushing a stretcher.

"How long has she been unconscious?" the first medic on the scene asked.

Ren and Raine looked at each other. Ren spoke up. "She called me about twenty-five minutes ago? We got here and called you immediately, having found her like this. She's a cop. A detective and my partner. Is she going to be okay?"

"She's lost a lot of blood. I think we got to her in time, though."

They put her on a stretcher and loaded her up in the emergency vehicle. As the ambulance drove away, sirens blaring, the forensics team showed up.

"I'm going to be here for a bit to make sure forensics gets everything they need. I'll get your prints tomorrow, if that's okay, Raine?"

"Yeah. That's fine. I'll be at the hospital with Apple."

"So will I," Feather interjected. "I don't know her, but I don't want to be by myself when someone you both care for is injured."

Ren moved over to Feather, taking her hand and pulling her outside to speak to her alone. "Are you going to be okay?"

"Sure. I didn't really know her, so this isn't about me."

"Not exactly. I know her and so does Raine. The injuries. They were similar to the marks left on the other victims."

"You mean Paige and Silver? They were clawed?"

"Yes, Paige and Silver. As for were they clawed? No. Not exactly. Their eyes were. It just can't be a coincidence about the claws."

"If that's the case, why didn't he kill her like them? Why didn't he take her eyes or burn her body? Not that I'm not grateful she is not dead, thank goodness, but, don't most killers use the same method?"

"Normally, yes. Shade's a fighter. He might not have expected her to put up such an effort. The others didn't have a chance to fight. There were no defensive wounds on them or anything to indicate they put up a struggle of any kind. That's not true here. The living room is a mess with broken furniture and window and stuff. No. He didn't surprise her as well as he had the others. He hadn't expected her to fight him and win. I think he jumped out the window to escape. Her gun was out, and recently fired. I think she just lost too much blood in the interim and he's unaware of the damage he incurred on her."

"I'm glad he missed the opportunity. Maybe when she wakes up she will remember what happened and you can catch him. Make him pay for Silver, Paige and all the others."

Ren stepped closer to her, cupping her chin. "Back at the camp, when I spent the night with you, I thought you were amazing. Seeing you again, after all this time, my feelings for you have only deepened. I want you safe. This guy, whoever this is, has been stalking you and eliminating anyone you seemed to care about or know. Eventually, he is going to get tired of his game and come after you directly. I need you to be safe until we catch him. I need to know he can't get you."

"I'll stay close to Raine when you're not around."

"Promise? Raine or me. You won't go off by yourself until we catch this guy?"

"I promise." She looked up at him, his hand still tucked under her chin, tilting her face upwards. His dark brown eyes filled with concern. He had always been kind to her, and the evening they spent just talking and allowing her to get to know him again only encouraged her to know more. She wondered what it would be like to kiss him. A warm, unknown desire spread through her body and suddenly that was all she could think about. Would he do it? Kiss her? Press his lips against hers? She had been kissed before. Michael and a few others from her past, but never much more than that. She hadn't cared back then if Michael or anyone else kissed her. She knew it was something they wanted and it seemed safe enough, so she let them. But, Ren was different. *She* wanted to kiss *him.* He didn't seem to move, as if weighing his options on whether it was too early to kiss or something. She decided to make the first move. Yes, it was something new, but she felt the need to take the chance and hope he wouldn't reject her.

When she met him years ago, it was unheard of for the woman to make the first move. However, since the '60s, it was totally acceptable. With a nervous hesitation, which lasted only moments, she leaned in and pressed her lips against his, her eyes closed. She savored the gentle touch before pulling back.

Ren wasn't ready to let her go, not yet. He moved his hand and gripped her shoulders, pulling her against him. He dreamed of this for a very long time. Somewhere in the back of his mind, she had always been there. Now, she was here in front of him and she *kissed* him. *She* kissed *him*! There was no way in hell he was going to let her go now. Or ever. A passion that had slowly been building since he had realized who she was outside of Paige's place had finally come to its head, and he wasn't about to let go. Not now. Not for as long as she would have him.

He crushed his mouth against hers, his longing for her evident. Ren's tongue begged for entrance and she gave it to him. He was in a heaven of his own making. Nothing could've been more perfect. Nothing, that is, except the surroundings and outlying circumstances.

Raine cleared his throat harshly, reminding Ren where they were and why. He leaned away, moving to kiss Feather's forehead. "I'm going to keep you to your promise." Without another word, he moved away, past Raine and back into the house where forensics was working on gathering all evidence.

"What promise?" Raine moved over to his sister, taking her arm to lead her back to his truck.

"I promised to not be alone. That I would stay by either you or him until the killer was caught."

Raine pulled Feather to a stop and spun her to face him. "Are you telling me he thinks the fucking wacko that killed your friends did this to Apple?"

She nodded. "He suspects it. He wants me to be safe."

Raine gave a single curt motion of his head and led her once again towards his truck. "Good to know. You're not leaving my sight and neither is Apple. I was going to drop you off at home first, but fuck that. We're going to the hospital. I'm not leaving either of you two alone."

Chapter Fifteen

Ren entered the hospital room. Raine was sitting by Apple's side, holding her hand. She was still unconscious and he guessed his partner hadn't woken up yet. His eyes glanced over to the monitors beeping softly in the background, then sought out Feather. She was in the corner, her eyes shut.

"She fell asleep about twenty minutes ago." Raine's voice was whispered. He didn't want to wake her accidently.

Ren moved over and grabbed a blanket from the closet, draping it gently over Feather. Raine watched him as he returned to the bed on the other side of Raine.

"You like her?"

Ren nodded. "I always have. I just didn't realize how much until recently."

Raine's brow furrowed. "What do you mean, you always have?" He knew because Feather had told him earlier that very night, but he wondered how truthful Ren would be and this seemed as good of a way to test him as any other.

Ren sat on the chair by the bed. "I mean, I met Feather when she arrived at the mountain camp. It was my duty to meet the train and bring the prospectives up to Xulth."

"Funny, she never mentioned that."

"She didn't recall until I reminded her just the other day."

"But, you remembered her?"

"Yes. To be honest here, Raine, she caught my attention the moment she stepped off the train. I had the chance to talk to her quite a bit at the camp and I really came to admire her. I hadn't realized until I saw her at the first vic's house how much she was still on my mind. Even after all these years."

"Must've sucked carrying a torch for her for so long and come to find out she hadn't given you a second thought."

"Not really. I didn't expect her to, I guess. I tried for a couple of years to find her, but she wasn't with her tribe anymore and I just didn't know where to look, so I gave up. I just never stopped thinking about her."

Raine was quiet for a while, his thumb rubbing the back of Apple's hand has he held it. He would have been beyond pissed if not for the fact he totally understood Ren at the moment. Had Apple just disappeared, he would look for her. But for how long before he gave up was an entirely different question. And he knew, deep down inside, he was fully aware he would never be able to get her out of his mind. She had a spunk, a no-nonsense approach to her that seemed to beckon to him in a way nothing ever had. She was like a little torpedo. One would think she was sweet and quiet and then, boom, she'd have you lying on the floor staring at the ceiling and wondering what the fuck just happened. He loved that about her, that unpredictability.

As long as she would let him, he wouldn't leave her side. However, the issue of Feather then came up. He promised his mother he would always take care of her, protect her. Yet, she was an adult woman in an era where women had equal rights and an equal say. They could buy their own property, go anywhere they wished, go on dates without a chaperone. The world had changed about them. Even the fact they were Native American no longer held the stigmatism it once had. The government was no longer trying to eradicate them with reservations, boarding schools, and cultural genocide.

Years ago, he would have chosen her mate, but again, times have changed considerably. She had the right to choose whom she wanted, not whoever was forced upon her. Even still, he had been cautious of who would be good enough for her, who would protect her. Maybe that was why he didn't want to give permission to Payne when he asked for Feather's hand. Payne had a cold harshness to him. Raine wouldn't take the chance of subjecting Feather to it and having her hurt or abused like his mother was.

However, Ren did not have that vibe to him. He gave off the sense of protector, of a caring person, and as much as Raine hated to admit it, of a man who could be in love. "The choice is hers who she wishes to be with, but if you are asking me? I would give my blessing."

Ren smiled. He didn't get a chance to respond, though, as Feather spoke up softly, her eyes still closed. "I'm right here. Don't be marrying me off without my input, brother."

Raine rolled his eyes, casting a backwards glance at his sister. "I said the choice was yours, Spud. Get over it already."

Feather yawned, her arms coming out from under the blanket.

Ren flushed, even his ears turned a bit red. "I was just saying, I'd like to keep seeing you."

"You're the only one who brought up marriage, Spud. You'll scare the first man interested in you off if you keep threatening him with such a harsh punishment."

"Good thing I don't scare easily." Ren stood and moved over to Feather. "How about I take you down to the cafeteria? We never got much of a chance to eat and you must be starving."

"What about Apple?"

"I don't think she is hungry."

Feather rolled her eyes. "I meant about leaving her. You just got here."

"I know, but Raine has it under control. She is still unconscious, so it's not like she will miss me. We won't be long. And, you need food. I can bring something back for you, too, Raine, if you want."

"Coffee would be good. Thanks. I'll stay with her. She won't be alone."

"See, all taken care of. By the way, because she is a cop and was attacked, there is an armed guard outside her door. I didn't want you surprised if you head out of the room for any reason."

"Thanks. That's good to know, but I'm not leaving her side."

"I didn't think so, but thought I would mention it." Ren gave a long look at his partner unmoving on the bed. Her complexion was almost as pale as the sheets she was lying on. "She's tough, you know. She'll pull through."

"The doctors said the same thing, but I'm not

leaving her until after she wakes up."

Ren nodded and held his hand out to Feather. "Let's go find the man some coffee and get you something to eat."

She slipped her hand in his. He was sweet to her, looking after her and conscientious of her needs, from keeping her company when she was frightened, to believing in her when she was accused of multiple murders, to now. He was a good man. No one cared for her as well as her brother, but Ren came awfully close.

Once they were alone, Raine stood and kissed Apple's temple. "Come on, baby. I just found you. Time to wake up and kick the ass of the one who did this to you. I know you want to. I knew from the moment I met you, you weren't going to be the one to sit idly by. You're a fighter. Fight this and wake up." He petted her hair back and waited. His eyes went to the monitors a couple of times. Blood pressure was steady. Oxygen level was steady. Heart rate was steady. They had replaced most of her blood, so why wasn't she waking up?

*   *   *

He moved the mop across the already clean floor; his eyes drifted to the room with the uniformed guard seated in front of the door. He looked away quickly, keeping his head down so as not to attract too much attention.

He hadn't expected her to be one of his kind. A shifter. That misstep cost him dearly. It was a mistake he would not make again. However, she had seen him. He couldn't afford to have her give a description of what he looked like to anyone. Especially them. It would ruin everything. Seventy years of planned work and torture would disappear immediately. If he were found out, he would have to up his timetable immensely and he wasn't prepared for that, either. All he needed was five minutes alone in the room with her. Five, and he can take care of her quickly. Everything would be on track, then. Everything would be good. He would forgo the ritual he had laid out for himself.

Stealing her soul. Eating her heart. But the eyes. The eyes could still be his. Slit her throat, take the eyes, leave. Simple. Just five minutes. All he needed. Just five.

Then she appeared, walking with the male cop he had seen before at the crime scenes. HIS crime scenes. Watching as things unfolded and they ran around like baboons, not knowing how someone could be so cold, calculating and disturbing. "How could one human do that to another?" he would hear them ask and shake their head in disbelief. If only they knew.

He grew up during a time when scalping a man was the natural order of things. When it was a way to gain their power. Eating the heart was a way to gain their strength. The eyes, they were the windows to the soul he now carried inside of him. They were reminders of the souls he harvested, the souls he was now a guardian for. They were better off in his care, for he would see no harm come to them.

His eyes narrowed as he noticed they held

hands. *Slut.* Turning his back to them, he pulled his hat down further and watched them in the reflection of the glass display case. Not surprisingly, they paid no attention to him as they walked past the guard and entered the room. He just needed to bide his time. Patience was one thing he had plenty of.

Chapter Sixteen

Apple moaned. "Did someone get the number of the truck that hit me?"

Ren jumped up and leaned over. "Not yet. Hey, Shade. How are you feeling?"

"Like I've been hit by a truck? Didn't the first thing I say register with you?"

Ren snorted. "Yeah, but since when do I listen to you?"

"Never." She smiled as she looked up at him and then around the room. There were a dozen plants and flowers scattered about.

Ren watched her for a moment. "Some are from the precinct. The huge ass bouquet of Sunflowers is from Raine. He's been here with you for hours. I just sent him home, not more than an hour ago, to get some sleep and a shower. The man was getting ripe."

"He was here?"

"Raine drove to your place when we found you. He's been at your side the entire time."

"How long?"

"36 hours. Did you see the guy?"

"Yeah. Didn't talk much, but I don't think he was expecting me being a shifter and matching his strength and prowess."

"Thank gods for small favors."

"He's an owl."

"You saw him shift?"

"No. My gift allows me to see things like that."

"Fuck. An owl. So, the truth behind the myths… Fuck."

"Yeah. Fuck." Apple closed her eyes again. She was weary.

"Well, we can't put out an APB on an owl. I'll get a sketch artist in here so we can get an idea of what we are looking for."

"Yeah. Although I would pay top dollar to see the Captain's face if we did put out one for an owl."

"Rest. I'll call the station and let them know you're awake and we need an artist down here pronto."

"Don't call Raine. He needs the rest."

"You sure?"

"Yes. Let him rest at home. I'll be here when he gets back on his own. If you tell him I'm awake, he will just rush down here and I don't need that."

"Alright." Ren pulled out his cell and walked to the other side of the room in order to give her a bit of peace so she could rest some more while he called the station with the news, as well as to request the artist. One would be there within the hour.

In the meantime, he sat next to her bedside, sipping the cold cup of coffee he had gotten before he forced Raine to take Feather back home and get some rest.

* * *

Ren looked at the sketch of the guy who attacked Apple. Once he downloaded a copy to his phone, he made sure it was sent out to the department. He walked the artist out the door and stopped to talk to the guard on duty, making sure he saw the picture as well. Not that there was much of a chance of him coming in, since the room had been limited to either the nurse on duty or her doctor. They didn't take any chances with a detective who had been attacked, especially after a big bust or as a result of current investigations, including that of a serial killer.

Payne was watching. Staying in the shadows, he waited for the opportunity to get into the room and not be discovered. She had yet to be left alone, making it difficult to get that moment he needed. He knew it would come. Yet, time was running out. He heard from the nurse she was awake. He'd seen another enter the room, one he didn't recognize. He didn't care. Well, maybe he did, a little, but he would deal with that issue, if need be, when the time came. He observed Ren and the stranger come out and talk to the uniformed officer. The unknown man moved down the hall and the other two moved away from the door. The moment he had been waiting for presented itself. He would not have the five minutes he had been hoping for, but even a couple of minutes were all he needed.

He slipped inside the room and locked the door. He turned to face her, but her eyes were closed. With a quickened step, he crossed the room to her bedside just as she opened her eyes, expecting to see Ren back in the room. She was about to scream, but his orbs focused on hers and she was lost to their hypnotizing effect.

He was so focused on bending her will to his, he was startled to hear the gun shots. The door was kicked open once the lock had been shot out. Ren and the officer both rushed in, breaking the spell he had Apple under. She was still too weak to do much of anything, but that didn't stop her from trying to sit up.

"Cobb, help her," Ren called to the officer. "I'll take care of him."

Apple almost growled at Ren, but she also realized the prudent measures he was taking with regards to her safety and the officers.

While Cobb assisted Apple in lying back down, Ren and the killer squared off. He tried to get Ren to peer into his eyes, but Ren kept his gaze away from the man's ocular tools of enchantment. He knew the battle was lost. Those couple of minutes he so desperately waited for vanished in a millisecond. He hadn't even gotten close to her, and now they all knew what he looked like.

Escape was his only recourse, and the window his only outlet. Ren seemed to know what he was going to attempt, as he tackled him to prevent him from departing. The two wrestled on the ground, knocking over a chair and table. Gifted flower baskets and vases toppled as the two men grappled with each other. Ren threw a couple of punches when he could and received just as many in return.

As others began to approach the room from the scuffling occurring inside, he elongated his talons and swiped at Ren, causing him to careen backwards at the foot of Apple's bed. By the time he regained his footing, he had burst through the window, shifting in midair and flying away. Ren ran to the opening and peered out, just in time to see a great horned owl flying away.

Ren growled in frustration, knocking over three more vases as he did so, then banged the wall with his fist. "Coward!" he yelled to the atmosphere. Hehoped the damned owl heard him.

Security personnel, a couple of doctors, Raine and Feather rushed into the room as a result of the chaos that could be heard throughout the entire wing. Raine didn't bother with anything else, other than rushing to Apple's side and pushing Cobb out of the way.

"You're awake! How are you feeling? When did you awaken? What happened? Are you okay?" He bombarded her with questions, but she couldn't answer so many.

Cobb ran to the window, surprised he didn't see a body down below. "Where did he go? We're four stories up, for Christ's sake. Where'd the perp go?"

Ren clapped him on the shoulder. "He landed in an open dump truck that was passing by just as he jumped. Go put an APB on it and deal with hospital security, please. I'll take care of the rest of this in here."

Cobb nodded, but looked out the window one last time, shaking his head in disbelief. He turned and left the room, taking the hospital security detail with him.

Raine backed up so the doctors could check and make sure Apple was okay, but once they left, he was back by her side. When it was just the four of them in the room, Feather shut the door, knowing they would want a little bit of privacy in order to talk.

Raine turned on Ren almost immediately, pushing him up against a wall, his hands fisted around his shirt. "What the hell, man. You send me home and don't let me know she woke up? You leave her alone and that manic tries to kill her again? You let him go? I ought to kill you, but it would break my sister's heart, though fuck knows why."

Ren shoved him back. "Get a grip on yourself. You know you needed the rest and so did Feather. I didn't leave her alone and I didn't fucking let him get away."

"You didn't? So, the fucker is under arrest? I don't see him. I see a bunch of broken glass from a window, and flowers and water all over the floor, but him I don't fucking see."

"Stop it. I told him not to call you. When he said you had been by my side since I came in, I figured you needed the rest. No one could predict what was going to occur. And he didn't let him get away. He tried to stop him. There is only so much a person, even a shifter, can do, especially in front of humans."

Apple's tone and words seemed to calm Raine down and he let Ren go, albeit reluctantly.

Feather moved over to the guys. "We have enough problems without you two fighting in a hospital."

"Hey, at least if the meatheads kill each other, they won't have far to go. Morgue is in the basement," Apple said, a sarcastic tone to her voice.

Raine moved back over to Apple. "Did you at least get a good look at the guy?"

"I did the first time."

"We had a sketch artist come in while you were gone." Ren pulled out his phone and brought up the picture to show Raine.

Raine's eyes widened and he snatched the phone from Ren. "No. No fucking way! This can't be!" He showed Feather the picture and she paled.

"We were told he was dead."

"Who? Who is it?"

"Payne. Payne River."

Chapter Seventeen

"I don't understand. How is this possible? I still have the letter by the Army saying he was killed. Even if they made a mistake, he never came home. I don't understand." Feather was totally distraught.

"Why would he go after Feather or both of you?"

Raine shook his head, then his eyes widened and he looked at Feather.

"What?" Feather looked around the room to find them all looking at her. "What? What did I do?"

Raine cleared his throat. "Um. Well. It's not what you did, it's what I kind of told him."

Feather's focus narrowed on her brother. "What did you tell him?"

"He asked my permission to marry you a couple of weeks before we were supposed to ship out for duty. I told him I'd discuss it with you, but it'd be your decision. The night before we were supposed to leave, he asked me if I talked to you."

Raine ran a hand through his hair. "I told him you weren't interested because we were headed out to war and you didn't want to make a commitment like that."

"So, what? He thinks I wasn't interested at all?"

"No. Not exactly. I think he knew I wouldn't give him my permission. Look. He was like a brother, but a cruel and sadistic one. I saw it every time we hunted or raided a party. He reminded me of Father, only he didn't need the alcohol to make him mean. I wasn't going to consent to that. Not for you. We'd been through enough with Father; I wasn't going to agree to put you with him."

"I'm glad for that. I didn't love him and certainly not in that way. But, even still, why go after the people we care about? Why not come home after the war? Why let us continue to think he was dead? I just don't understand any of this."

Raine moved to her at the same time Ren started to, but Ren held back instead.

"Look, Spud. Why he didn't tell us he was

alive, or didn't come home, only he knows the answers to those questions. As well as why he's doing all these killings. Even as an owl, he specifically went after those we knew and cared about. It's not random, it's specific."

"Raine's right, Feather. Whatever reasons he's on this killing spree, or whatever set him off, is in his mind. I'll tell you from experience, in most cases, to a normal person, it won't make any sense. Serial killers tend to be in their own world of right and wrong. Sometimes, they even believe they are saving the world, or the person, or voices are telling them to do it. Whatever, it's not your responsibility or fault as to why he's no longer playing with a full deck. What is important is finding him and preventing him from killing anyone else."

Apple spoke up. "Anything you can tell us about him—his personality, his likes, his hunting style—anything will be helpful for us to catch him."

"You mean us, not you, to catch him. You are going to stay here and heal." Ren folded his arms in a no-nonsense position.

"Just as I'm not leaving, even for a cup of coffee, until he's caught," Raine put in. "I'm not having you put at risk again."

"I don't want Feather by herself, either. If he can't get Shade, or you, he might decide to go after what he really wants, or wanted. Feather."

"You really think he'd come after me?" Feather looked around at the group, wide eyed.

"No offense, baby, but I truly think you're the reason he has been killing. I'm not sure exactly why, but all the evidence points to something with you. He has been eliminating your friends, your acquaintances, your past lovers. And, he has been moving closer so you have noticed it, noticed his deeds, and thereby noticed him. Paige and Silver were just the latest steps to getting closer to you in a long line of manipulative moves on his part."

"Oh, gods. All of them? Whatever reason he is doing this, it's all because of me they are dead?" Feather stood and started to pace, her hand over her mouth as nausea began to twist her insides. If she had only known, maybe she could have prevented so many deaths. If only she knew why he was after her, maybe she could stop it. If onlys, though, were a hard pill to swallow when one blamed oneself, even if she didn't understand why she was feeling guilty.

Apple spoke up. "Feather? Serial killers are warped. There is something psychologically wrong with them, and feeling guilty or shouldering the blame does nothing but make you feel bad for the deeds of another. Raine and Ren don't deserve that, and neither do you. If you start blaming yourself for another's deeds, you might as well blame Raine for it, and in due course, an argument can be made for Ren and me. The dude is a nut job, and I'll not partake in the position I asked for it, or I'm to blame."

"I never said you or any of them asked for it."

"No, but it is the logical course of feeling guilty."

"Shade has a point." Ren moved over to her and rested his hand on her shoulder. "If you start to think about yourself as being the cause, then you'll go insane. Don't blame yourself for another's issues. Ever." He moved away and pulled out a pad and paper. "On the other hand, you can do something. You can tell us everything you know about him. It might lead to us finding him."

"And if it doesn't? Then what? We keep Spud under a watchful eye for the rest of our lives?"

"No. We use her as bait." Ren was confident in his words, as if he were saying men from Mars just landed on the White House lawn and no one could broker a different opinion.

"Are you out of your cotton-picking mind? No fucking way are you going to use her as bait! Are you daft? Let her be used to lure a serial killer? I think you're off your fucking rocker. And here, I was just beginning to like you," Raine growled low, infuriated Ren would even consider something so dangerous.

"I'm not stupid. You think I *want* to use her or put her in danger? I'd rather cut off my arm than see that happen, but the truth is, she's in more danger if we do nothing. Eventually, he's going to go after the cause of his obsession. In this case, his obsession is Feather. If we use her, we can protect her better," Ren snarled back. He turned to look over at Feather, a deep sadness in his chocolate eyes. "We're going to try everything else first. It will only be as a last resort. I don't want to put you in any danger, Feather. I want to make sure my partner remains safe as well."

The room was very quiet for a few moments, the only sound the monitoring machine's beeps.

Raine broke the silence. "What do you need to know?"

Chapter Eighteen

Payne paced over the already tattered rug in his small, one-room apartment. This wasn't going the way it should've. He should have eliminated Detective Shade the first time he tried, in her home. Yet, he admitted he was startled to find she was a shifter, or that she had overpowered him, even momentarily.

And then there was Detective Shaw. His blood boiled at the thought of seeing Feather and Shaw holding hands. He grabbed the alarm clock and threw it against the mirror of his dresser, shattering the glass. How dare she let him touch her? Didn't she figure out yet that she was his? But then, why would he expect anything different? She and Raine moved on with their lives, not even caring about him.

Did they look for him after the Battle of the Bulge? Did they worry about how he was doing? Did they come to visit him in the hospital while he was recouping? Or in rehabilitation for three years?

No! When he did get released, three years after the war ended, he had to hunt them down. And what did he find when he did? They had already left. Probably because they knew he was coming and didn't want him to find them. He tortured and killed their old apartment manager to get an idea where they might go. That was the first time he killed because of her, and he would continue to do so in his constant search.

Somewhere along the line he decided it was time to kill them both. Remove all her friends first, then her brother. He would save her for last and enjoy every delicious morsel she would provide. He would devour every bit of her, capture her power, her essence, and her life force. She would live in him since she didn't want to live *with* him.

However, things had changed drastically, and he needed to make some alterations to his original plan. Since he failed at eliminating the female detective, he'd have to go after someone else first. He was well aware the two detectives had seen him and would probably make a sketch of what he looked like. He no longer enjoyed the anonymity he had since the end of the Second World War. He pulled out his pouch, opening it up and taking out the eyes he had taken over the years. Some were beginning to rot. Other, more recent ones, still held the look of surprised pain as death came upon them.

"She is why you are here. Do you think she has been punished enough?" Payne asked them, walking around the room. "I don't. But what am I to do?"

He stopped and stared at the rotting orbs on the table. "Do you think?" Payne tilted his head, listening to only something he could hear. "You're right. Of course, you're right. I should've seen it sooner. I was blind." Payne started to pace again, then stopped, nodding at the eyes. "Yes. That's what we'll do." He gathered up the eyeballs and stuck them back in his pouch. He was clear for the first time in a while on what he needed to do next.

*   *   *

Three days and Apple Shade was healing nicely. She was never left alone, but then neither was Feather. Both Raine and Ren made sure of it. Three days of watching over the women and talking. Getting to know each other more, feelings that had started to develop before, deepened.

Things had been quiet at the hospital, and talk of Apple being released in a couple of hours was the current discussion. Apple wanted to go back home, but technically it was still an active crime scene. Anything she wanted from her own place she would have to buy or do without. Raine wanted to bring her back to his place, which he shared with his sister. Ren wasn't too crazy about that until Raine invited him to stay there as well. Then, suddenly, Ren was all for it.

"What is it about paperwork that seems to take forever to get so one can leave?" Apple grumbled to the nurse about the discharge papers she would need, as well as some follow-up doctor appointments and some meds in case she needed them at home. "I just want to get out of here."

The nurse departed the room to finish retrieving everything and call for a wheelchair.

"Cool your jets, Shade. Raine doesn't even have the truck to the door yet and you still need shoes."

"Well where the hell are they?" Apple looked around.

"I got them." Feather held them up to show her. "And here I thought doctors made the worst patients. It's cops."

"No. Just Shade. She never had much patience."

"Like you do, Shaw?"

"I never said I had patience." Shaw moved to the door. "The nurse is coming back with the rest of your release papers. Take a chill pill."

Apple slipped on her shoes, finishing up by the time the nurse returned with the wheelchair and final papers. She signed the last of her paperwork and stood to leave. Ren pointed to the wheelchair for her to get in. "Hospital policy."

"Tough shit. I'm not getting in that thing when

I am perfectly capable of walking."

"She really is stubborn, isn't she?" Raine commented as he walked into the room.

"She won't get in the chair." Feather moved towards the door with Ren, who held her hand whenever possible.

"We know you are rough and tough. You don't always need to prove it. Tell you what. Either you get in the chair and ride down as per hospital rules, or I will carry you over my shoulder the whole way." Raine crossed his arms, his body taking up the bulk of the entryway.

Apple glared at him for a few moments, the nurse standing to the side behind the chair watching between the two as if it were a tennis match. "Fine." Apple stormed over to the chair and got in. Nodding, Raine stepped back and let the nurse push her down the hallway to the elevator, the rest of them following.

Chapter Nineteen

Raine led the group into the house; Ren was the last to enter. Each of them carried a couple of plants and flowers. There had been so many for Apple to bring from the hospital, they each had to carry them in.

"You can have my room, but I think the flowers should be scattered around the living room. There is more light there." Raine dropped the two he was carrying, then headed to his room to drop the shoulder bag with the few items Apple had from the hospital. When he turned, she was in the doorway. "Make a list of the things you are going to need or want and we can get them for you."

"I'm not an invalid. I can go shopping, you know."

"No. You're not an invalid, but you are still recovering from an injury where you suffered major blood loss. Anything you need, we can get for you and you can spend the time being lazy and resting. Watch TV, whatever. I have a great set up in my room."

"And where are you going to sleep?"

Raine looked a bit uncomfortable at first. "I can sleep on the floor."

"In here?"

"I'm not leaving you alone, not even in this room. Ain't happening." He folded his arms, waiting for her to put up a fight on this subject.

"Why don't I just take the floor?"

Raine rolled his eyes. "Really? You have to ask? Let me spell it out for you. 1. You're a guest in my home. 2. You're recouping. 3. You're a woman and I would never let a woman sleep on the floor when there is a perfectly good bed available. And 4. Because it's my room and I insist, as my guest, you get the bed." He leaned forward as if daring her to refute him.

"You're not going to sleep on the floor."

"I'm sleeping in this room. You don't like it, tough shit."

"Fine, but you're sleeping in bed with me."

Raine pulled back, shocked. He was not

expecting that whatsoever. "What?" he stammered, uncertain. She caught him totally off guard.

"You're sleeping in bed with me," she said matter-of-factly, brooking no argument. She reached up and pulled him down, pressing her lips to his.

At first, he stiffened. A millisecond later, he wrapped his arms around her and lifted her off her feet. He really liked the modern age and women taking the lead. There was no question when they did so. He walked with her legs dangling against him before wrapping them around his waist as they neared the bed. Their lips remained locked as he moved; he carefully laid her upon the bed. She unhooked her legs. After a few more kisses, he stood and looked down at her. "Tonight, I won't stop. For now, I still have to unload the truck and you have a list of things you need to work on." His voice was deeper and huskier than just moments before.

He breathed a moment, manually shifting his throbbing cock around to give it some comfort as he looked down at her. He didn't want to stop. He wanted to take her right now and seriously considered it. "Fuck." He was going to forgo the whole thing and take her, but just as he took a step forward, Ren poked his head in.

"Hey, just got a call from the precinct. A caller claims he saw Payne near the Riverwalk by Crockett Street last night. I want to go check it out."

"Not alone." Raine was grateful for the interruption and getting him to think just a bit more clearly.

"You aren't coming, if that's what you were thinking. You need to stay and protect the girls. I'll have backup. I'm meeting Lt. Ortiz and a couple of others to canvas the area. Should only be a couple of hours or so."

"Why do you have to go?" Feather came up behind Ren, peering through the doorway and getting the distinct impression they just interrupted Raine and Apple.

Ren turned to look at her. "Because I'm a cop and I have to do something. Especially if it can keep you and Shade safe."

Raine moved the two of them back into the living room. "Go. I'll watch the girls."

"Great. I'll only be a couple of hours at most."

Feather walked with him to the door, catching his arm to stop him for a moment. Raine discreetly moved back into his room to give them a moment of privacy.

"You'll be careful? I don't want anything to happen to you."

Ren lifted his hand and caressed her cheek. "Yes, beautiful. I have you to come back to." He leaned over and kissed her lightly, then quickly departed so he wouldn't change his mind.

She watched him a moment before re-entering the house and locking the door behind her. Something just didn't set right with her about his leaving, although, admittedly, she was probably just concerned for his safety. Over the past couple of days, she had grown to care for him greatly. Even though she hadn't said anything to him, or he to her, she was sure the feeling was mutual.

Raine looked up as she came back in. He was in the living room with Apple, shoving a tablet and pen at her to write down what she needed. Turning to his sister, he gave her a reassuring smile. "He'll be okay. Don't worry."

Apple looked up. "My partner is good at what he does and he doesn't take unnecessary risks. If he has a chance to find this guy, he'll take it."

"I know. I'm probably just being silly, but I'm worried. Payne was always unpredictable, and now? Now I just don't know."

Raine moved over to his sister and tilted her chin to get her to look up at him. "You can't think about Payne. Ren isn't going to take risks. He won't want to chance not coming back to you. He likes you too much."

"Do you think so?"

Apple piped up. "Shit, girl. It's all over his face the moment he sees you. Ain't never seen him so into someone as he is with you. I actually thought he was gay for a while. Guess he was just waiting on you, though."

Raine cocked an eyebrow, the left side of his lip crooking upwards. His little spitfire. He kept his eyes on his sister. "See. He's liked you for far too long to do anything that'd screw it up. As Apple—"

"Shade." He was cut off when she called out.

Raine tossed her a look and finished his sentence. "As *Apple* said, he's never been happier than when you two are together. I've seen it, Spud. And you look just as happy." He touched her lips gently. "See. There's that smile with just his name or thought. I don't think I've ever seen that before."

Feather moved to hug him. "Thanks, bro."

Raine squeezed her, then let her go and went back to Apple, who was still giving him the stink eye.

"I hate the name Apple. Don't call me that."

"Nope. The world can call you Shade or whatever, but you are the Apple of my eye and I will call you Apple." He kissed her wrinkled brow and chuckled, pulling the tablet from her hands to see what she had written down.

"Fine, but only you. Anyone else even tries and

I will kick their teeth in."

Feather shook her head and entered another room, quietly leaving the two of them together.

Chapter Twenty

Where are you? Payne asked, his mind sending out the request. She was a strong-willed woman, but nothing can beat his power. Once he was inside her mind, he would always be there. Nothing would change that. *Where are you?* he cooed into her mind once again. This time, he got an answer and he smiled.

He finished up his preparations, then headed out. He saw them. Talking to passersby, to those in the area. He knew they were looking for him, hoping to find out where he was, hoping to capture him. He snorted. He was smarter, better than all of them put together. They would never find him or where he was going to keep her.

Walking along the Riverwalk in the opposite direction, he mingled with the crowds that abounded there. Fools, all of them. They never even saw him. He was invincible.

*   *   *

Apple came out of Feather's room. She was almost robotic in her movements, but her mission had been accomplished. Feather stopped her as she exited the bedroom. "Were you looking for me?"

Apple blinked and looked around. "No. I don't think so. I must have just taken a wrong turn. Sorry."

"No problem."

"He'll be back soon. Don't worry."

Yet, Feather was worried. He said soon, but that was four hours ago, and no word. She just wanted to know what was going on and that he was okay. Her head snapped up at the knock on the door and she almost ran to it. She flung the door open, then ran into his arms when she realized Ren had finally returned.

He held her as he walked her backward so he could get in the house and shut the door behind them. "Missed you, too." He kissed the top of her forehead before letting her go as Raine and Apple came into the foyer.

"Any luck?" Apple asked.

"None. Anything to eat?" Ren pulled off his jacket and slung it over his shoulder, unsure what to do with it.

Feather came over and took his jacket, laying it across the chair in the living room. "Sure. I saved you some stew. Let me heat it up for you while you fill us in on your search."

Heading into the kitchen, Feather grabbed a bowl from the cabinet while she turned the stove back on to re-heat the stew she had made earlier. She pulled out some cornbread muffins and placed them on a bread plate, handing it to him, then turned back to the stove.

Apple and Raine came in and took seats at the table as well, waiting for Ren to start talking about the search.

Grateful for the muffins and the bowl of stew Feather gave him, he took a couple of bites before he started to talk. She put a bottle of beer in front of him, then took the last empty chair at the table as she sat. Since the three of them just finished eating before Ren came, she was pretty sure none of them wanted anything else. Except, of course, information and the capture of Payne.

"There were about six of us. Three teams of two with Payne's picture trying to get some information, but no go." He shook his head, spooning the stew into his mouth and chewing on the chunks of meat and potatoes. "We spent four hours asking everyone we came across. One guy, we think the one who called it in, thought he looked familiar, like one of the boat drivers, but it wasn't him after all. We went up and down Crockett Street, but nothing. He probably was never there, but who knows. Tourists don't pay much attention and those that might've seen him were probably long gone to another area of interest or shopping or something." Ren banged the bowl with his spoon a couple of times before he looked up at Feather. "Sorry, babe. Not this time. We'll have better luck soon. I just know it. He can't hide forever."

Feather reached across and laid her hand on his holding the spoon. "I have no doubts you'll find him. I'm not worried."

"It usually takes about 100 tips before one reliable one comes in. This is normal police work. Not quite as glamorous as on TV," Apple pointed out.

"We had this one other lead, the original caller. He said he saw him going into the old Aztec Theater, but most of that is now shops and restaurants. There is a bit of remodeling going on, but nothing that would make a good hiding spot for him, so if he went there, it might have just been in passing."

Feather looked over at Raine with a perplexed look on her face. "The Old Aztec Theater? The one built in 1926?"

At first Raine didn't catch it, but after the look Feather gave him it clicked for him, too, and he turned to await the answer.

"Yes." Ren's head swiveled between the siblings. "What? What are you just now remembering?"

Raine scrubbed his face and turned to Ren.

"Just before the war, Payne, Feather and I came to San Antonio. We heard about work here and it seemed like a good place to move to. A growing city, we could get lost before we started to attract suspicion for not aging. They needed men to dig out the Great Bend of the canal. It had to be dug out in some places or filled in at others in order to equalize the seven-foot drop of the bend and make the Riverwalk a reality. The WPA was brought in on March 29, 1939, with funds raised from the DAR to beautify the city.

"Although the Aztec Theater had been built back in 1926 and wasn't near the bend we were working on, a number of us who didn't have a place or means to get one stayed in some of the lower-level rooms of the theater. Robert Hugman, who was the designer of the area, had plans to put restaurants and shops in the rooms we were staying in. But because we were also working on the canal, it was a project that was put on the back burner for a few years. By the time it was ready, most of us had moved away to other locations."

Feather took over the telling of the story at that point. "Thing was, even though we found a couple of places by the old missions to stay, Payne was fascinated with the rooms below the theater. He once told me, if the war ever broke out and the Nazis ever came to the U.S. to go to the theater and hide, it would be able to survive the bombs. Now, I know it's below street level, but I never understood how it could survive the bombs. If it went any further down it would hit more water and the rooms would be flooded. So, it never made much sense to me, but I also forgot about it. When the war broke out, both Payne and Raine joined the military and got shipped out. I joined the Red Cross. Every now and again we would get reports, threats of an attack, whatever, and we would go to bomb shelters, but I always wondered about the one at the Aztec Theater. When it became Aztec on the River, I figured the shelter, or whatever it was, disappeared too. Yet, now I wonder… I mean, maybe he is there. Using it as his base of operations or whatever. Maybe that's why he hasn't been found."

"Could be, but I doubt it. Those shops and restaurants have been there for almost over 80 years. Surely someone else would have found them in all this time?" Finishing his meal, Ren sat forward, wrapping both hands around his bottle of beer.

"I don't know, but the location is an awful strong coincidence. Being who and what we are, coincidences are not necessarily something I take for granted. Neither should you." Raine watched Feather take Ren's bowl, tipping it in silent offer to refill it.

Ren shook his head no, giving her a soft smile before getting serious again as he turned back to Raine and the conversation at hand. "I can take a couple more officers tomorrow to check it out, see if we can find this bunker you heard about, but honestly? I'm not sure it still exists, if it ever did."

"Payne was a lot of things, but he wasn't a liar. At the time, he considered us family. He wanted to help protect us. He was in love with Feather, or so he claimed. I can't see him lying to us. Not then.

Not when he thought it could make the difference."

"Fine. Let me call the Captain and set up another search of the area tomorrow." Ren pulled out his cell and dialed, explaining what he needed. Disconnecting the call, he laid the phone on the table next to his beer. "We're meeting at ten for another search. Maybe we'll be lucky this time."

*   *   *

Raine realized Apple was getting tired. She had, after all, just come home from the hospital. Wishing the other two good night, Raine helped Apple into his room. He gave her a few minutes of privacy, in order to change and get ready for bed, while he double-checked all the doors and windows to make sure they were locked and secured. Feather and Ren were still talking in the kitchen, but now about other things instead of Payne. They were talking about a possible future for themselves and he was grateful to see his sister so happy. Ren was a good man. He would treat Feather well. And with her happily taken care of, Raine could focus on a woman he was interested in. One that was currently waiting for him in his bedroom and who already established he was going to sleep in the same bed as her.

She was still healing, though, so he would keep his dick in his pants and just hold her. Until Payne was captured, he had no intention of not being by Apple's side making sure she was protected. When Raine finished up checking the house, he knocked softly on his bedroom door.

"Come in. I'm about as decent as you're ever going to get."

He smirked and opened the door, stepping quickly inside. His smile vanished immediately, his mouth going instantly dry and all his blood flowing to his nether regions. Slowly, he let the door close behind him, but otherwise barely moved. He was awe struck by her beauty as she lay sprawled out on his bed in an alluring pose and a very short, slinky, satin-and-lace mini-gown. The outfit clung to her curves and outlined her shape perfectly.

"Apple," he moaned, his eyes darkening immediately.

She didn't say anything, but patted the empty space next to her on the bed, her posture silently asking him to join her.

"Apple," he bemoaned. "Don't."

Her hand went up to her bodice, then slowly caressed downward, grazing lightly over her breasts. She didn't need to ask if she was affecting him. The sudden bulge in his pants, the slight beads of sweat on his forehead told her everything she needed or wanted to know. She was having the desired effect on him. She smiled beguilingly and patted the bed again.

"Apple." His cock throbbed in desperation to be set free. She was a temptress he was having an extremely difficult time resisting. He should walk out the door and sleep on the floor in front of the bedroom, or on the living room couch facing the door, which he would keep open. Anything to refuse to give in to what she was asking of him. Men were supposed to be the ones to make the first move, but his little spitfire was a woman who took matters into her own hands, and that made her even more desirable as far as he was concerned.

He hadn't even realized it, but he was standing next to the bed, his hand reaching out to caress her bare shoulder and the thin spaghetti strap that lay upon it. He tried to remember why he couldn't touch her, shouldn't take her. Shit, she was offering herself up to him and he should turn her down? What the fuck was wrong with him? "You're still healing."

"I'm not as bad as you think. You know our healing abilities are better than humans. My guide also helped speed up the process. At best, I'm a little stiff, but I'm sure you can help work out any rigidity I'm still experiencing." She didn't move, letting him contemplate her invitation to its full measure. She had always taken what she wanted, went after whatever she craved. Right now, she wanted Raine. At this moment, she craved his body with hers.

"I can't protect you this way."

Apple reached down and rubbed the bulge in his jeans, her eyes on his. "I don't want protection. Especially not from you. Not tonight."

He couldn't deny her or himself any further. He pushed her back as he climbed on top of her, careful to not hurt her. Leaning down, he took her lips with his. "Apple! You're a very wicked minx."

Her hands were already on his belt, undoing it with a quickness he didn't think possible. In moments, she had his belt and his jeans undone. Slipping her hands underneath the material, she pushed the harsh denim away from his skin and down his legs until she could go no further because of his kneeling. He moved off her and kicked his shoes, socks and jeans off. Pulling his shirt off, he climbed back in bed, lying along the side of her, fingering her spaghetti strap.

He was beyond asking if this was what she wanted, beyond denying what they obviously both craved. He slid her strap down, letting his fingers caress her skin as he pushed the top of her gown off, exposing her breast. Her nipple was already hard, but he knew that from the indentations it made before he moved the thin material away. He kissed her lips lightly, tilting her head to the side and pushing her short hair away to tug on her ear with his teeth before he trailed his kisses down her throat. She was still partially covered, the other strap holding one side in place. He moved it down, licking his lips as he admired her perfectly curved breasts. He leaned closer to blow his hot breath on one mound, watching as her eyes fluttered, a sigh escaping her lips.

Raine flicked his tongue around her nipple, enjoying how much tauter it had become. His other hand easily cupped her, massaging her. The scent of her arousal hit him and made him even harder, something he didn't think was even possible. He wanted to go slow, enjoy every delicate morsel she was providing and make sure he didn't accidentally hurt her. He wanted to give her hours and hours of pleasure, restraining himself only to see the look of passion on her face repeatedly. He moved his lips to her other breast and taunted her without any mercy.

Apple's hand played with his long, silky hair, then pulled it roughly, almost like she was going to pull him away from her body. Instead, she held him close to her breast. Her leg slid over his thigh, rubbing against his eminent erection, and he groaned in ecstasy. He moved his free hand down her ribs to catch her leg, lifting it higher on his hip, his fingers biting into her ass. He planned on tasting every inch of her. He knew before this night was done, he could never let her go.

Apple had other plans, though. She moved her hands down to his chest and pushed him back, straddling him. She pulled the short gown over her head and peered down at him. "Tear them off. Rip them."

Raines eyes traveled over her body, coming to rest on the thin material that separated his access to her sweet core. He gripped the lace panties in his hands and pulled, hearing the satisfying rip of the undergarment tearing. He tossed the shredded linen aside and gazed up at her. Having a woman take control like this was super sexy and his cock throbbed even more.

She rubbed her wetness on his shaft until he was well lubricated, then she plunged him into her body. His hands were on her hips and he arched to meet her downward thrust, moaning at how good and tight she felt around him. She stopped and he had to open his eyes to see what had happened to still her. She was gazing down at him. When she saw he was watching, she moved, her breasts bouncing with her actions.

Apple was taking her own pleasure from him, something he was certainly not used to, and something he found highly erotic. He let her lead their session. There would be plenty of other opportunities for him to take control, but tonight, their first time, he relinquished it to her.

Her muscles tightened around him as she gripped his long hair tightly, twisting it in her fist. She came, her juices coating his rod as she paused a moment to let her convulsions subside slightly. When she was ready, she moved again. Only he stopped her. He sat up and flipped her onto her back, her legs now up in the air. A look of surprise was clearly on her face as she stared up at him. "My turn, little spitfire." Raine pushed himself up, spreading her legs wider apart and looking down to see himself buried to the hilt inside of her. He moved once, pulling his glistening cock out, then slowly buried it deep within her heated core. He pulled out a second time while moving her legs up towards her chest. In one swift movement, he released her legs and flipped her onto her stomach. Grabbing her hips, he pulled her ass up and plunged into her without hardly missing a single beat.

Raine leaned over her, his arms wrapped around her. He reached under and played with her breasts as he continued to pound into her body relentlessly. Her hands gripped the sheets as she groaned. The sound of flesh hitting flesh excited her. "That's so good. Don't stop."

"I don't have any plans of stopping, especially right now." He let go of one of her breasts and slapped her ass, leaving a nice red handprint on her pale skin. He held her still for a moment, both hands on her hips as he leaned over and kissed her between her shoulder blades. With her on all fours, he was at the perfect vantage for admiring her tight little ass and his own shaft shining with wetness from her juices. She didn't seem to mind the slap, and the idea she would let him use her to get off excited him in a way he didn't think possible.

Raine reached around and rubbed her clit as he began to thrust into her. He wanted her to come again before he allowed himself his own satisfaction. Her nub was hard, and the way she squirmed as he played with it told him it was also a bit tender. "Come for me," he commanded, increasing speed and intensity to get her to cry out beneath him.

Moments later, she obeyed his verbal directive. Her head dropped to the mattress as she cried out with the magnitude of her orgasm. He was glad she came, because if he had kept up that pace much longer, he would have joined her and he wasn't totally ready for that just yet.

"One more time," he whispered into her ear,

then kissed just below it.

She knew exactly what he meant, what he wanted from her. He was buried deep inside, and taking her with him so as not to fall out, he shifted his legs to wrap in front of her as he pulled her back, keeping her on top of him in a reverse cowboy. He was sitting with his chest against her back, his hands on her front. One hand was touching her clit again, the other playing with her nipple. His head was buried in the crook of her neck, kissing and nipping at her ear.

She stilled his hand at her clit. The almost painful reverberations would set her off far too soon and she knew he needed to build up again just as she did. When she knew the break she needed was enough, she released his hand. "Now," she commanded huskily.

He didn't waste any time. Raine began to rub her nub and tweak her nipple while she bounced up and down on his extremely hard rod. He could feel his balls begin to tighten. He had punished them enough by making himself wait, but no more. He needed to fulfill his desire, needed to claim her body as his. He really liked her and maybe that was the difference. She was strong, determined, stubborn, a spitfire who lived up to the name he gave her. She took what she wanted, when she wanted it. She brooked no arguments and could fight equally well as he did. If he admitted it to himself, he might even go so far as to say he was falling in love with her. Regardless, the depth of feelings she brought out in him made this session unique to any other he had been with over the multitude of years. His heart warmed that she chose him and he wasn't ever going to betray that.

He pinched her nipples and her clit hard, then moved his hands to her hips, aiding to increase her motion. Her hand curled under his balls and she massaged them as she rode him. Her other hand reached over her head to grab his hair against his scalp and pull on it. A thrill of excited ecstasy went through him. She knew exactly what she was doing to him and he couldn't be more surprised at her experience, or more grateful than he was at that moment.

A sheen of sweat broke out on both of them and he felt his dick swell within her. He was very close. He needed to know she was, too. Her sounds were becoming more rapid, more intense, and he knew. "That's it, my little spitfire. Come for me one more time. This time, I'm going to join you in bliss. Come for me. Now."

Those words pushed something inside, her body immediately responding. She leaned her head back on his shoulder, her hand giving him one last squeeze of his balls and pulling his hair so hard his own head tilted back. He growled as he jerked into her, his hot seed crashing against her womb. She shivered against him, everything relaxing a few moments later.

He all but forgot she had been injured until that moment and his concern for her increased as his hand gently checked on her ribs' wounds. "Are you okay? I didn't hurt you, did I?"

Turning her head to do her best to see him, she gave him a large grin. "The hurt you inflicted was fucking awesome and I'll do it again when you're ready."

He laughed. Yep, there was his little spitfire. Oh, he was going to enjoy every part of her flesh, and maybe even her heart and soul, many, many times. Slowly, he laid back, taking her with him, spooning her as he rolled them over to their sides. "If you let me, I'd like to claim you." He was nervous. He never felt so scared of being rejected, but then he never asked to claim someone before, either.

"That's just great sex talking," she mumbled against his arm as her head rested on it. She had no doubts of this just being a sexual encounter, a next step of their budding relationship. She didn't expect it to go much further, at least not immediately.

He lifted himself up to peer down at her. "Yes, the sex was awesome. I'll admit that, but my asking you has nothing to do with it. Well, not entirely. It was awesome because I actually feel something for you. You're not just a lay to get my rocks off. I care for you greatly, Apple. I want to spend a lot more time with you, and not just having sex, despite how fucking amazing it is."

She looked up at him, astonishment clearly on her face. She never expected this from him. She liked him, too. A hell of a lot. She respected the fact he treated her well, considered her needs and her feelings. No guy had ever done that before. Ever. They used her and moved on. It was why she took the initiative tonight. She assumed once Payne was captured, she wouldn't see Raine again. There would be no need. So, she took the steps to have something that would last for her. A memory that would be with her for a very long time.

Her eyes searched his for a few moments, then she gave him a small smile. "Tell you what. Stop calling me Apple. I really hate it. And see what you feel like when the afterglow is gone. We can discuss it in the morning. Fair enough?"

"Fair enough." He had no plans on changing his mind, but he understood that asking her right after the first time they made love—yes, made love. Not had sex, but a real deeper connection—was not the time to claim her without her worrying it was only because he got laid.

He settled back down behind her, wrapping his arms around her and closed his eyes. Morning could not come soon enough.

Chapter Twenty-One

Her eyes snapped open, albeit they were a bit unseeing. *Open the door,* whispered in her head and she was compelled to obey. Listening to Raine's heavy breathing, she knew he was sound asleep. Carefully, so as not to awaken him, she slipped out of the bedroom and shut the door behind her, taking no chances she would disturb him. She could see Ren on the couch in the living room, his body facing the open door to Feather's room.

He wasn't her concern. She had a directive and her feet softly padded to the house entrance. She removed all obstacles barring the door closed and flung it open. A great horned owl stood on the stoop and, taking flight, flew into the house as she held the door open. She stood at the door, unmoving, unresponsive. The owl soared into the house, shifting easily into human form. Payne sent a silent question to Apple, who in turn indicated the open door in front of Ren.

Payne strode into the room and looked down at

his sleeping prize. She was even more beautiful when her features were not encumbered by the events of the day one deals with when awake. He bent down and scooped her up. In her unconscious state, her arm and head dangled from his arms as he turned and walked out of the house. He stopped only a moment at the open doorway where Apple had remained.

His gaze went over her naked body. He could smell Raine on her and knew the two had sex. Lots of intercourse from the smell of it. "I should've killed you," he whispered, more to himself than anyone else. "Glad I didn't. You make a much better mole alive than a symbol of their continued downfall." He gave her one last glance, then headed out with Feather still unconscious in his arms, sending a silent message to Apple to lock the door and go back to bed.

*   *   *

Ren couldn't remember a sleep that deep in,

well, ever. He stretched on the couch and stood, feeling still a bit groggy. He headed to the bathroom to do his morning ablutions before going to the bedroom to check on Feather. Her bed was empty. Panic took hold and he ran to the kitchen. Not there. He moved with haste about the house but could find no trace of her. Ren was beside himself. He pounded on Raine's door, flown open within moments by a none-too-happy, sweatpants-wearing Raine with Apple tucked under the covers, pulled up to her neck to hide her own nakedness.

Unlike Raine's furious glare, her eyes were worried. She knew her partner too well to know he wouldn't disturb them unless something was majorly important. "What's happened?"

"Feather. She's missing."

Raine's jaw clenched. "What do you mean missing?" He shoved Ren aside and moved to her room. His path followed something akin to Ren's just minutes before, going around the house in desperate search for his sister. He sent a mental link to her but there was no response, which only served to worry him more.

Apple used the distraction of the guys searching to slip on a pair of pants and a white shirt before leaving Raine's bedroom and looking around as the guys began to panic.

"Where the fuck is she?" Raine was ready to punch something, and since Ren had taken responsibility to protect her, he would do nicely.

Something caught Apple's eye and she headed over to pick it up, paling as she did so. "Guys?" She held out an owl feather.

"How the fuck did he get in? Or by you? You were supposed to be watching her."

Ren grabbed the feather, turning it around in his fingers before he glared back at Raine. "I thought you locked all the doors and windows. I slept on that couch all night, facing her open door. I have no fucking clue what happened. Maybe you should have been listening instead of screwing all night."

Raine threw a left hook, knocking Ren down. He stood over him and glared. "Don't ever say something like that to me again, asshole. I entrusted my sister with you."

Ren rubbed his jaw as he stared up at Raine. He was about to jump to his feet and tackle Raine but Apple stepped between them. "Stop. You two can see who has the bigger dick later, as well as play the blame game. Right now, we need to assume Feather has been taken by Payne. Since he didn't leave her body here, we might also be able to assume she is still alive and needs us, not two pussy willows playing the dickhead ego game. Shaw, call this in and get the search moved up. Raine, check the windows and doors and see if you can figure out how he got in. I'm going to get my shoes and gun. Then the three of us are going hunting."

Without another word, she turned her back on them and headed back into the bedroom. The two guys watched her for a moment, then turned back to each other. Raine held out his hand to help Ren up. A small smile twitched on the left side of his mouth.

Ren grabbed Raine's hand and got up. "Nice punch. Don't ever fucking try it again." He looked after Apple. "You've got your hands full with her, you know."

Raine's twitch went to a full, outright grin. "Yeah. I know."

Ren pulled out his phone and called the station, bringing them up to date about the kidnapping of Feather and putting a rush on the search.

Raine turned and checked all the windows and doors again. They all were bolted shut, except the front door had one bolt left undone. There was a drop of liquid in the doorway and it puzzled him. He bent down to test it with his finger and bring it up to his nose to sniff. His frown deepened and his stomach turned. He turned to face the two of them as they approached, ready to leave.

Raine's eyes darkened in fury. He grabbed Apple and flung her against the wall opposite the door, his hand squeezing her throat. "How could you?"

Ren pulled out his gun, not entirely sure what the fuck just happened. "Let her go. Now. Or I'll shoot."

"She did it. She let him in the fucking front door. She *betrayed* us both."

Apple squirmed in his grasp, her hands clawing at his hand squeezing her throat and cutting off her oxygen. "What the fuck are you talking about?" She would have kicked him in the balls, but he was pressed up tightly against her, giving her nowhere to maneuver.

"Did you have fun? Making love to me over and over so I just passed out in exhaustion? You should have cleaned yourself. Washed me off you! Did he tell you to screw me first to put me off my guard? To make it easier to stab me in the back and help him take my sister?"

Ren held his gun aimed at Raine, but he was listening and looking at his partner, unsure and waited for her answers.

Raine didn't give her a chance to respond. With his free hand, he stuck his finger under her nose. "That's us. The results of our pleasure. Found by the front door, that wasn't totally locked the way I left it yesterday. Oh, you screwed me so well last night I didn't even comprehend it until now."

She paled and stopped struggling. Her eyes became wild as she struggled to comprehend she might have done this. "Raine. Baby. I wouldn't do this. I wouldn't. I don't remember. I fell asleep and don't remember anything until Ren pounded on the door. Please believe me."

"Fucking bitch. Every word out of your mouth is a lie. You can't deny the evidence."

Ren holstered his weapon and laid a hand on the arm Raine was using to squeeze Apple's life force. "Actually, Raine. It might not be a lie."

Raine's only movement was to turn his head to look at the detective. "Explain."

"Payne's an owl. You have heard the stories as much as I have. I never believed them much, but…" He looked at his partner. "He tranced her in the hospital. If he can do that, and he can age the organs by stealing their souls, who's to say he can't also continue their trance and bid them to do whatever, as per the legends."

Raine hesitated. "So, you're saying, he tranced

Apple once, and he can put her under with just a thought now that he has been in her head?"

"According to myth, and all myths are based in fact. You know, deep inside you know, Shade would never betray you or Feather. She wouldn't do this."

"That's right. I wouldn't. I didn't fuck you to throw you off your game. I did it because I wanted to. I wouldn't help that fucker if I was paid to. I didn't do it, or if I did, I didn't do it consciously or on purpose. You gotta believe that, babe. I swear it's the truth."

No one moved or breathed for a few moments, then Raine released her. He still didn't trust her, but he let her go. Spinning, he flung the door open and headed to his truck. "Let's go."

She called after him. "Shoes, Raine. You need shoes and a shirt."

Raine didn't stop as he made them appear on his body without missing a single stride. Ren copied the action for his own preparedness as he quickly stepped out the door. Apple shut the door, shoes, weapon and badge in hand, as she ran to catch up.

Chapter Twenty-Two

Several police cars had blocked off Crockett Street by the Aztec theater. A couple of police boats were on the river, making sure the barges kept moving and the area otherwise remained off limits.

Raine pulled up in his truck, Ren and Apple both flashing their badges so they could bypass the barricade. Finding a place to park, Raine closed his eyes again, attempting to contact his sister. Still no response, which told him she was either still unconscious or dead. He sincerely hoped it was the former.

Raine looked around as the three headed for the stairs, which would lead them down to the Riverwalk and the eating and shopping complex there. Both Apple and Ren grabbed a police vest and additional weapons from one of the other cars. It bothered him Feather was gone and he couldn't contact her, not even through their mental links. It also disturbed him that Payne had his hooks into Apple and could get her to do things for him anytime he wanted. Why not have him tell her to shoot her partner or him? Or any one of a hundred different innocents? True, it wouldn't be her, just her vessel, but she would have to live with the consequences for all the years after.

Apple didn't seem to like the loss of her free will any more than he did, from the looks of it. She was in police gear—black pants, white shirt, black police vest—her short hair was pulled back in a small ponytail and she wearing dark sunglasses. Fuck, she looked hot. However, this wasn't the time to admire his no-nonsense little spitfire. He had to find his sister and know she was okay.

It didn't help that Ren seemed like an overwrought basket case, and Raine thought he was bad. But then, if positions were reversed and it was Apple that was missing, he would be pretty freaked, too. Hell if he already wasn't. He tried the mental link again, then growled in frustration when he couldn't contact her.

Ren gave him a look of 'what's up?' Raine scrubbed his face and lowered his voice.

"Frustrated. Spud and I share a mental link and she's not responding."

Ren stopped dead in his tracks. "I should've guessed, but fuck me sideways. There are so few, I just never gave it a thought. No word though?"

"None."

"Doesn't mean anything. Probably still unconscious." Which, of course, made Raine frown more. While they had been getting ready to head out, Apple realized she was missing some sleeping pills to help her counteract her pain. There were six missing. They soon realized she must have put two in Ren's drink and four in Feather's to get them to sleep so soundly. She might have even put one in Raine's drink, but they couldn't be sure about that, either. In truth, they couldn't be sure about anything when it came to Apple being under the influence of Payne.

In truth, she should not even be there. She hadn't been cleared by the psych department after being injured, nor had the doctors fully cleared her for duty. On top of that, she was a liability since she was currently influenced by Payne to do whatever he wished. Yet, she wanted the opportunity to find Feather. Even though she was not fully at fault, she felt responsible for her disappearance. She hated being used. Hated it with a passion, and if she got the chance, Apple was going to show Payne exactly how much.

They arrived on the Riverwalk beneath the old Aztec Theater. It had been a while since Raine had been there and he looked around trying to take in all the changes. He had to admit, Hugman's vision of a beautiful, park-like area with shops and restaurants finally came true after years of planning and raising funds. All worth it in the end. It was a definite boon for the city, attracting tourists from all over the world. A mini-Venice of Spanish, Mexican and Indian heritages. What started as just an idea for a few blocks in the downtown area now stretched over fifteen linear miles from Brackenridge Park to Mission Espada, the farthest of the five historic missions in San Antonio.

Raine tried to remember where the rooms were

located that they used to employ while working on the WPA project, digging out the canal, but so much had been altered. It took him a few moments to get his bearings.

Ren and Apple seemed to understand he was trying to get reacquainted with the area despite all the changes. Then it seemed to click and he headed over to the corner wall. Start with something small, unchanged, and go from there.

Raine hated he couldn't just shift and try to find them as a lion. He had the feeling Ren felt the same way, but a cougar and a black bear walking around the Riverwalk was a sure invitation to get themselves tranquilized and stuck in the Brackenridge Zoo. Unfortunately, there were far too many humans for them to just use their senses, everything instead just became muddled and indistinguishable.

At the corner of the building, he followed the inside wall. Ren and Apple followed his lead. Very few were in this area, all busy talking to others or searching more logical places. None of them had been here back in the late '20s and early '30s. None of them knew about the hidden rooms that were once dressing rooms for the live actors for the stage above. The Aztec was almost laid out like catacombs, with several alcoves along the way. Many had been closed off or even bricked up, but there was a back way to access them. Walking around what was familiar reminded him how to find the hidden entryway.

Apple looked behind them, making sure no one else was watching, yet at the same time, making sure the other officers were nearby. Just in case.

"Help me." Raine called to Ren to help him move a filled bookcase. He may be shifter strong, but even he had his limits.

Ren came over and together the two of them moved the heavy piece of furniture. Raine smiled a look of success. Looking around quickly, he found the release lever and the panel slid open, revealing a narrow hallway with several doors. Although much had been undisturbed over the years, as indicated by a heavy level of dust build-up, there was an area that showed more recent usage. Raine didn't wait. He moved rapidly to the door and flung it open. Ren wasted no time entering behind him and Apple followed both men.

It was empty. Albeit, there was evidence laying around that Payne had been there. Pictures of Paige, Silver, Uxem, Austin, Raine, Ren, Apple and several others were plastered up on a wall. Some of the pictures had a red circle around the face and a large X through it. From their records, the ones with the Xs were those who had been killed. However, it was the other wall that concerned them the most. The whole wall was plastered with pictures of Feather, some dating back to the 1940s as she was attired in a Red Cross uniform. Others were more recent, including one where she is holding Ren's hand.

Ren pulled out his walkie talkie and let the others know where he was at and to have forensics come immediately.

"She's not here. Where the hell did he take her? How are we going to find her now?"

"We will, Raine. I don't know how yet, but we will find her. We're going to go over this entire place with a fine-tooth comb. Somewhere he will have left something behind to give us a clue where they are now. There is too much here to have been totally abandoned. We'll find her." Ren almost growled the words out, though whether convincing himself or Raine, he had no clue.

Chapter Twenty-Three

Feather slowly became aware of her surroundings. It was dark and she was a bit cramped. She tried to wipe her eyes and found herself bound to a headboard. She took a moment to look around and figure out what was going on. She was still in her nightwear, and she realized she was no longer in her own bed but somewhere else.

Suddenly, she realized what happened, and just as the thought came to her, Payne walked into the room.

"Good morning, beautiful. Although, technically, it's early evening."

"Where am I? Why do you have me tied up? Payne, how are you even still alive?"

"You're with me. I've got you tied up because you'd try to run away and I just can't have that. Don't try to shift, either. The cuffs are made with feldspar, which, as you know, prevents the use of our powers. Now, how I'm still alive, that's a very good question." Payne pulled up a chair next to the bed, sitting on it backwards, his arms folded over the edge of the chair. "Are you telling me you never knew I was alive?"

Feather tried to sit up, but her bondages prevented her from doing so. "I got a letter from the government stating you died in Europe. They even sent me one of those gold stars to stick in my window. Even though that was technically for mothers who lost their sons and daughters in the war, I guess they felt I qualified since we were your only family. We were told you were dead."

He was quiet a moment, tapping the chair with the tip of his elongated fingernail. "I've never known you to lie to me, Feather. Never, that is, UNTIL NOW!" he yelled as he stood and tossed the chair angrily to the side.

"I'm not lying now. I've never lied to you. Why do you think I'd start now?"

"Because I don't believe you. I don't think you thought I was dead. I think you left me when I needed you the most." He paced, his anger in his words as well as his heavy footsteps.

Shifter's Pride

"Payne. What happened to you?"

"What happened? What *happened?* I'll tell you what happened. I woke up in a hospital alone with no support, not even a fucking letter. The explosion that went off from a tank hit the wall of a building I was using as cover and the wall fell on my legs. I went through months of rehab to regain the use of them. Did I ever hear from you or Raine? Hell, no. Not once. I stayed in Europe for a couple of years after the war. I figured if you didn't want me, I sure as hell didn't want you." He scooped up the chair and sat back down again in the same position. "Did Raine tell you I wanted to make you my mate before we shipped out?"

She shook her head. "No. He didn't. He did tell me recently about it, though. He said he told you he'd talk to me about it, but felt we were too much like siblings, and with you both shipping out for the war, he didn't feel it right to have me answer you. If I said no, you'd have been hurt and not focused on staying alive. If I said yes, and something happened to you, as we thought it had, it would've been devastating to me. Raine felt either way was a no-win situation. He told me it was something we'd have discussed when the war was over and we were all back together again. Decisions could be made with clearer heads then. I agreed with him. I think he made the right choice. Since we were told you died in battle, I think he was even more right."

"Bullshit! Why? Why do you keep lying to me?" He stood again, this time leaning over her on the bed.

"I'm not, Payne. Why won't you believe me?"

"Because you and your brother are adept liars. You think I have not noticed. I came back and every time I tried to find you, you had already left, trying to stay ahead of me so I wouldn't find you. How stupid do you really think I am?"

"At the moment, very. Why can't you hear what I am saying? Why can't you believe me? Raine and I have always been there for you. We took you in, treated you like family. Why do you think it would've changed because you went into the war?"

Payne climbed on top of her, his hands around her throat. She knew what he was capable of and shut her eyes immediately. She wasn't about to look into them and lose her very essence. "If you're going to kill me, just do it already. You've already taken away so many I cared about and even a few that were just acquaintances. What made you think that was okay?"

He growled, gave her another good shake before he got off her and stormed out of the room leaving her alone. She opened her eyes and took a deep breath of relief. She looked around the room, listened, and breathed in as much as she possibly could. She tried to shift, but cuffs were stopping her.

Raine? Can you hear me? Raine?

Spud? Thank gods. Where are you? Are you okay? Is Payne with you?

He just left the room. I'm not sure where I am, but I can't shift.

What do you see? Smell? Hear? Anything to help pinpoint where you're at?

Beer. I smell a lot of hops, like in beer production, but it also smells old. Feather looked around trying to get a better impression of where she was. *It's an older building. I heard banging earlier, like workers. Occasionally, I could hear people talking as they seemed to walk by. There is a lot of space. The walls are stone. I don't think I'm being much help.*

You're doing good, Spud. We're going to find you. Don't worry. We'll figure it out. Just stay safe for me. Contact me with any more clues. Don't give up, Spud. Don't. Do whatever it takes to stay alive. You hear me? Whatever.

Yeah. Whatever to stay alive. Just...hurry.

*   *   *

Raine turned to Ren and Apple. "Feather is still alive. He has her somewhere old, smells like hops or beer, stone walls, sounds of construction and groups of people going by on occasion. Any ideas?"

At first, they were all stumped. Ren pulled out

a map of the city from one of the police cars and brought it over to the truck. "I'm going to assume he hasn't taken her far, so let's see if we can find something that fits all of those clues she gave us." He put the map on the hood of the truck, scanning it. There was the Pearl Brewery, but that had been revamped into shopping, restaurants, the Cooking School of America and apartments. There also wasn't any construction going on that he was aware of. Blue Star and Freetail Breweries are too new to be old, though both were by the Mission district where there was a good deal of construction. "Oh, wait." Ren and Apple looked at each other. "Lone Star," they both said at the same time.

Ren turned to Raine. "The Lone Star Brewery was built between 1895 and 1904. The facility is close to an old train depot near the east side of the city for easy rail transport, though it's not been used in years. There are many brick and stone buildings, which are on the property in order for it to handle the beer empire of Lone Star, which at one time was the largest brewery in Texas."

"The complex closed in the '70s, but the San Antonio Museum of Art opened in the '80s," Apple added. "The city council just approved a three-hundred-million-dollar plan to turn the rest of the brewery property into something similar to Pearl. They are also going to add a concert area, but the neighborhood is worried about noise pollution and parking. This just got passed last year, so there is still a lot of controversy going on."

"And you know this how?"

"I'm one of the ones in the neighborhood that will be affected. Anyways, they have been doing some construction, and since the museum is there, which also educates some art students on occasion, and hosts special events and banquets, that could account for the voices she heard."

"It seems to be the only one that fits everything she sensed or described."

"Then, Lone Star we go. However, I have one more concern. Spud said she can't shift. Any idea why? I've never heard of anything like that happening before."

Ren frowned. He had no clue what could prevent someone from being able to shift. He looked over at Shade to see if it resonated with her any. She pulled out her phone. "Let me make a phone call. I know someone who might know."

"While you do that, let's head over to the brewery and see what we can do in the meantime about finding her. If I can't shift, I can still tear Payne apart with my bare hands, or rather my cougar claws." Raine walked around the truck to the driver's door.

Ren folded up the map and got in the cab, as did Apple who sat in the middle as she waited for her party to pick up the phone.

"Hello Jackson, I'm sorry to bug you but can I possibly talk to Elder Sky? It's important."

The men remained quiet as they drove to the San Antonio Museum of Art. The old brewery was a fairly large complex, so accessing it from the museum seemed the most logical. It was going to take time to cover the property, but Ren didn't want to call the others to help search in fear of spooking

Payne. He had the distinct feeling Payne had seen them around the area the previous day, asking about him and showing his picture around, causing him to relocate. He wasn't about to take that chance again and endanger Feather unnecessarily.

Apple spent a few minutes talking to Elder Sky, explaining the situation. She then asked if he knew of a remedy. Making a few notes, she thanked the Elder and disconnected the call.

"Well, the elder had a couple of suggestions as to what could've caused the lack of shifting abilities. He thinks the most likely culprit is Scurfpea, also known as Texas Plaines Indian Breadroot. It's an herb and part of the pea family, non-toxic and not usually used for anything other than as a part of the wildflower beautification project Lady Bird Johnson started back in the '60s. Or she has some feldspar on her."

"Are either permanent?" Raine asked.

"No. However, it's going to take its sweet time to get out of her system if it's the former. Elder Sky said it could take up to two weeks. It's an inhibitor, but other than that, it's not harmful. If it's the latter, just take whatever it is off her."

"Like not being able to shift isn't harmful?" Raine rolled his eyes. "At least it's not poisonous or anything."

He pulled into the museum parking lot and shut the motor off. "Where do we start?"

"I'm not sure. Thing is, I fear if he sees any one of us, he will get spooked and we could lose them both again. Yet, I fear for Feather's overall safety as well." Ren scrubbed his face.

Apple looked between the men. "Look, I'm not crazy about this idea, I'm just getting this out there, but, I might have a plan. I'm just not sure it will work."

"I'm all ears, Spitfire."

"You got a thing for nicknames, don't you?" She grinned at him.

"You won't let me call you Apple, and I sure as hell ain't calling you Shade, so, yeah, I guess I do."

"What's your idea, Shade?"

Apple took a deep breath. "Okay. So, we figure

he used me somehow to unlock the door and let him in and fuck knows what else. So, what if we reverse it?"

"I don't understand." Raine was not at all pleased where this might be going. The last thing he needed was to worry about the girl he was falling for on top of already worrying about his sister.

"Well, I'm thinking if he can put me back in that hypnotic state and give me orders in my mind, why can't I try to back track that connection and get in his mind."

"Are you completely off your rocker, Shade? You'd be going into the mind of a serial killer. Who knows what will happen?"

"Shaw, what choice do we have? Spend hours walking around here and hope we come across where he has her? Hope he doesn't see us first and book? Or worse, feel he is being closed in on and kill her before we can stop him? I don't even know if I can do it. I've got to try. Don't you see, I have to try."

Raine turned in the cab and grabbed Apple's

shoulders to turn her and face him. "You're incredible." He kissed her hard while Ren got out of the truck and looked up at the museum and the old brewery in the background.

When Raine and Apple joined him, he pointed. "I figure she is going to have to be in an area they either completed or won't be worked on for a while, so as not to be discovered. It's also going to have to be near the special events center, otherwise she wouldn't have heard those other voices."

"I'm going to try and see if I can touch his mind. Maybe it will give us a better clue as to where he is holed up. I'm just not sure how to do this."

"What if you try to go into a trance and think about seeing things through his eyes?" Raine was throwing any idea out there he could. He was getting very concerned for Feather.

"Has she contacted you again?" Ren asked, concern buried within his voice.

"No, and I'm worried about contacting her again."

"You think he knows?"

"Honestly, I have no idea. I just know I don't think I've ever been more fearful than I am right now."

Apple put her hand on his arm. "Then let me try."

Raine looked down at her. "I'm not happy about this. Just so you know."

She nodded and turned to Ren. "Call for silent backup. We're going to need to move quickly on this."

"Already done while you two were smooching it up."

Apple took a deep breath to calm her nerves. "Here goes nothing." She closed her eyes and tried to go into a self-induced hypnotic state.

Several minutes later still nothing happened and Raine was getting more and more anxious. He was about to give her five more minutes, then he was going to rip every door off its hinges and he didn't care who he disturbed. He was *going* to find his sister.

Four minutes later and Raine was about to give

up when Apple suddenly became stiff and robotic. Turning, she started to walk across the street and into the museum. The two men quickly followed her. Ren ran over to the admissions desk, explained this was a police matter, showed his badge, and caught up to Raine, who was still following Apple. She went out the back door, past a couple of workmen and into another secure area that had been cordoned off. Ren pulled out his gun and cautiously trailed after them, indicating Raine, who was unarmed, should take a step back.

Raine gave a vehement shake of his head and continued to stay close to Apple. He realized the workmen were not in this area, nor were any guests of the museum. One step he was a man, the next he was a mountain lion—quiet, stealthy and lethal.

The shift surprised Ren, but he continued to follow Shade, who was deep in the trance. She opened another door and entered a larger room. The room was empty, save a table, chair and some miscellaneous items. On the table, however, was a horrific sight. Thirty-two eyeballs in varying degrees of rotted states, all of them staring at the new comers. Apple moved to the table and stood still.

Ren held his weapon aloft as he skirted about looking for Payne. There was another door in the corner. Lion Raine charged the door, crashing through it.

"Crap," Ren swore and ran after the large feline, leaving Apple behind. He wanted to call for backup but there was no chance with Raine running amok in his shifted form. Ren entered the next room and stopped short. Lion Raine had Payne on his stomach as he sat on his back. On the bed nearby, Feather was struggling to get up, relief on her face at seeing Raine and Ren.

Ren held his gun out with one hand and pulled his phone out with the other. He quickly called for backup. Before he finished the call, Raine had shifted back to human and pulled Payne up by the scruff of his neck. "How could you?"

"How could *you?*" Payne spat back. "You left me in Europe. You left me to die."

"How do we break the trance Shade is in?" Ren called out, the gun still on Payne.

"I kill her." Payne laughed manically. "Willing to do that now for you." He was silent a moment, and Apple walked into the room, still in a trance. She turned to Ren and kicked the gun out of his hand.

Raine wanted to help her, but if he did so, he knew he would be putting them all in danger, so he remained holding onto Payne. However, he hit Payne upside the head, stunning him and breaking the hold he had on Apple. Shade blinked and looked around, slightly stunned.

Police soon surrounded the room, bursting in. "Freeze!" one of the uniformed men yelled. Ren pushed his jacket back to show his badge on his belt. Apple was still in her police vest. Ren scooped up his weapon and moved to put cuffs on Payne. Raine moved over to Feather to keep her company while they looked for keys to unlock the chains she was in.

Ren had been prepared; pulling a sleep mask

out of his pocket, he put it over Payne's eyes. "Don't take that off him." He handed the cuffed prisoner to a couple of officers he knew he could trust with odd orders.

Apple found keys on the table with the eyes in the other room and brought them back to free Feather. She still had a lot of unanswered questions, but she didn't care about them anymore. She was safe and Payne was locked up. When the others cleared out and forensics were called in to catalog everything, Ren moved over to the others.

"Are you okay?" His concern for Feather was prominent.

She nodded. "I am now."

Raine had let her go and Ren gripped her tightly against his body.

Raine repeated the motion with Apple. The four walked out of the museum. There would still be a number of things to deal with in the coming days, but for now, they were all safe.

Chapter Twenty-Four

Raine went through security and was led to an open booth with a phone on the wall. He sat down and waited. It had been three weeks and this would be the first time Raine had a chance to see him. Or the courage. They had made sure Heller's Marbleseed was given to him each day. They told the warden it was his medicine, and though it wasn't entirely true, it was the only thing that would keep them safe from Payne's piercing, mesmerizing gaze. They also made sure he had the Texas Plaines Indian Breadroot to prevent him from shifting and possibly escaping.

Raine had too many questions. Questions he needed answered and inquiries humans couldn't be aware of. Despite his better judgment, Raine came to the prison to see Payne. He waited as the guard brought him in and set him at the table opposite Raine, the glass dividing them. After Payne picked up his handset, Raine reached to get his and put it to his ear. Honestly, he wasn't sure where to begin so they spent the first minute just staring at each other.

"How's Feather?" Payne figured he best say something, though he wasn't entirely sure why Raine would even visit him.

Raine scowled. "She's good. Happy, but let's leave her out of it."

"Fine. Let's get to the crux of the matter. You didn't bother with me after the war. Left me to rot in a hospital in Europe. Why are you bothering with me now?"

"First, let's get a couple of things straight. I was in a different area from you. I was a code talker and we didn't know what infantry were up to or where. We passed the information along when we got it, but if the commanding officers chose to ignore it, that was not our fault. So don't fucking blame me for what others did. We were told you were dead. Simple as that. If we had even one inkling you were alive, I'd have left no stone unturned searching for you and bringing you home. Why would I bother to look when we were told you died in battle?"

Payne just glared. "You didn't ask for a body? Wonder where I was so you could bury me? Maybe not having a body would've given you some inkling that maybe there wasn't a body, because I wasn't dead."

"Maybe, but it was in the middle of the war. I was deployed in another area of service than you. Spud was working at home for the Red Cross. Things were confusing and hectic. Not like we forgot about you intentionally. Just assumed the government buried you over there like they did at Normandy." Raine scrubbed his face. They could go around and around with this, and no matter what was said, Payne had it set in his mind they abandoned him. Nothing was going to change that. Ever.

"Look man, you're my blood brother. We went through a ton of shit together. Why'd you do it, man? Why'd you start to go after all our friends and acquaintances? Why just those you killed? What made them so special?"

Payne sat back in his chair and gazed at Raine.

He was quiet a moment, judging where to begin. Or how much to tell Raine. Even he wasn't sure. Finally, he decided to tell it all and suddenly felt like the villain in some B-Flick where he spills his guts to the hero as to why and how. Only Payne was not some B-Movie villain, he was a hero in his own mind, doing what he thought was important and needed. He saved those people. He should be thanked, not condemned.

"In rehab, I met this nurse. Fiona Zestrum. She took really good care of me after I was torn up from the building falling on me, causing my legs to not work. She was sweet, made me forget about Feather and you not being there for me. Made me feel wanted."

"That's great, Payne. Where is she now?"

"Dead. I killed her."

Raine frowned, saddened by this news. "Why? Why would you do that when she was so good to you? When you liked her?"

"I asked her to marry me and she jilted me. She took the ring and then broke it off. Made a promise and reneged." Payne's eyes darkened with his fury at remembering. "She broke my heart, so I took hers."

"What happened to you?"

"She was my first, you know. I don't mean the first kill. You and I did that quite a bit, killing settlers who interfered with our home, threatened our livelihood. Killed soldiers who tried to kill us first and scalped them all. It was our way. This is no different. Why does it bother you, when this is the natural order of things?"

"In the 1800s it was the natural order of things."

"You don't think it still is? Look at the wars, the constant fighting, the bombers who blow themselves up along with everything else, and you don't think killing is not the natural order of things? We just do it better now, more efficiently. Only, we don't get the power of our victims anymore. Bigger and better weapons than our knives and rifles, but that's the only difference. We haven't evolved from killing, we've enhanced it, made it more proficient."

Raine shook his head. "You're sick, dude. Seriously. So you killed Fiona because, what? She turned you down? Because you think it's the natural order of things that when someone pisses you off, taking their power is the right thing to do?"

"It's the only thing to do. I hadn't planned on killing Fiona. I saw red at her rejection. I hated her for making me feel for someone else, only to be spurned, just as you and Feather did. The difference is, this time I'd do something about it. I caught up with her, took her soul. Now she lives in me. I will never be without her, and she will never be without me," Payne said proudly, lifting his chin in triumph.

"You killed her."

"No. I gave her soul rebirth and I ate her heart for power. For her strength. For her love."

"And the eyes? What the fuck is up with those?"

"Reminders, mostly. Entrances to the soul that I now carry inside me. A way to bring a particular soul up and have them be a part of me again. When I look at them, I can feel them inside. I can remember the taste of their life essence. I can relieve those moments when they became a part of me. I guard them now. I protect them. I gave them eternal life and the eyes help me remember all who are entrusted to me."

Raine felt ill to his stomach. "You're fucking sick, dude. I mean, really. You're so far out of it, we need the fucking Hubble Telescope to find you. Do you really believe all that bullshit you just spewed my way? Or expect me to? Shit, man. We practically grew up together. In the boarding school, meeting up at the foothills of the training camp. All those years you lived with us, I knew you were harsher, more depraved than most, but I figured it was because of your losses. No family. We became your family. What the fuck, man? What the fucking fuck?" Raine scrubbed his face as he continued to hold the handset to his ear. He should never have come, but he had to know. Curiosity definitely killed this cat. Worse, he was a glutton for punishment. He asked his final question, hoping he had enough stamina to stay and listen to the answer.

"Why us? Feather and me? Just because you thought we didn't care?"

"Started out that way. Hatred for you both. For you not telling her I wanted to be with her. Doing so basically screamed you didn't want me as part of your family. Her not holding onto hope that I was still alive. After Fiona, I came back to the States. I had nowhere else to go. No one I wanted to be with. No one else I considered family. When I met your landlord just after you left, she was cruel to me. Said you were all better off without me and she didn't even know me! How could she think I wasn't good enough to be with you, unless you told her. Gave her a reason to believe I shouldn't be with you. I realized your friends and acquaintances need to be taught lessons, and at the same time, given something they couldn't have otherwise. Eternal life in me. Eventually, I would've confronted you and Feather. She would've been mine and you'd either have been happy for us or been in me and enjoyed it from there."

"And if she didn't want you? Didn't love you

that way?"

"Then she would've lived in me, too, and we'd never be apart."

Raine stood and slammed the handset down on the holder. He had nothing more to say to this beast in a man's skin.

The guard came back over to Payne, leading him back to his cell.

Chapter Twenty-Five

It was over. Finally over. For the first time in days—no, weeks—Feather felt like she could finally breathe. Payne was in prison, safely tucked away where he couldn't harm anyone else. Ren had kept his promise to her. He had protected and saved her, just as he said he would.

He led her to her room, instinctively checking it out. "All clear."

"Will you stay with me again?"

"There is no reason to, baby. It's safe. He won't ever hurt you again."

"I don't want to be alone. I'm still frightened."

Ren touched Feather's hair, tucking it behind her ear in a gentle caress. "I'll never let any harm come to you."

"I trust you. You've already saved me from him. Please, stay."

Ren pulled his hand back, turning towards the door. "I can't, Feather. Don't ask me. I don't have the strength to stay and not take you. It was easier when I had a job to protect you. I could focus on that. On keeping you safe, but now? No. I'm the only threat you face now."

"It's a threat I willingly accept."

He turned towards her. He couldn't help it. She touched his heart in a way no one else ever could, or ever did. Her amber eyes called to him and he would succumb if he stayed. He wanted to leave, but his feet had other plans. He was in front of her again, toe to toe, gazing down into those eyes that stole his breath away. "Feather. Please, you don't know what you are asking of me. I'm a man. I can only be so strong before I falter. You're pushing my limits. I'm about to fail. If you ask me to stay, I can't promise to be honorable. Not anymore." His voice was thick and husky with his growing desire. He needed to leave, and soon, but his feet refused to move. His hand, however, lifted to caress her smooth cheek.

Feather leaned into his touch. "I'm willing to be with you. Don't leave me. Please. I know what it means. I accept your terms. Just know that I've never been with a man before, Ren. I am not sure what to do."

Ren pulled back slightly, his heart pounding so hard he was sure it would just burst out of his chest. "No pressure, Feather. I'll never do anything you don't want me to do. Just say no and I'll always stop."

"And if I don't say no?"

"Look, baby. We will take everything slow. You call the shots. I've waited over a hundred years for you. I'll wait for as long as you want me to. You're in control and I'm good with that."

"I'm scared I'll do the wrong thing. Or that I won't be good and you won't want me again."

He laughed lightly. "Feather, my love. That won't ever happen. And do you know why?"

She shook her head no, clinging to every word he said.

"Because I love you. It's not just an act, not just two naked bodies moving in a rhythm to get off. It's about sharing our very beings, our souls. Making love and having sex are two very different things. You get me excited for more than just sex. I've loved you for a very long time. If it was only sex, then yeah, I might say that you did it wrong or you were horrible at it, but it's not sex. It's making love. It's an opportunity for me to share the next important part of myself and what you give me. It's a complete sharing of what makes us who we are and accepting the other with all their flaws. No one is perfect. I sure as hell am not and I don't expect you to be perfect in everything you do, especially when you have never done it before. You will learn. I will teach you. Baby, you are a lioness. And I will do my damnedest to make you roar. If you let me."

She didn't say anything. She didn't have to. He said more than enough for the both of them. She gave him a slight nod and let her trembling fingers slowly unbutton her blouse. He took a step closer, putting his hands on hers.

"Are you sure?" He would never push her, never force himself on her or make her feel guilty if she said no. This was her decision. He would abide by it. He just prayed she wouldn't tell him to stop.

She smiled and nodded. "I want this. I want it with you. For all the reasons you've said. It's more than just sex. I want to show you how much I'm in love with you."

He grinned. He looked like the Cheshire cat who caught the fattest mouse in the village. He jerked her against his body and ravaged her mouth with his kisses. He couldn't get enough of her as his hands tore her shirt off. Ren would buy her a new one tomorrow. His fingers worked on undoing the bra binding her. He wanted her breasts free and to be able to taste her skin, feel her nipple harden in his mouth. He was going to take it slow, explore every bit of her body and commit it to memory. He knew he was going to do his best to get his lion to roar over and over again before the night was over. He was going make her first time one to remember. He planned on having this night be so special to her, she would willingly give herself to him repeatedly. He was going to be her first, and he desperately wanted to make sure he was the last.

He managed to get her bra off and tossed it

aside on the floor with her torn blouse. He looked down into her gorgeous amber eyes, hoping she was okay and hadn't changed her mind. He lowered his mouth to hers, the kiss more intimate than ever before. His hands caressed the smoothness of her back until he hit the waistline of her jeans. Ren bent down and took her breast in his mouth, savoring the taste of her skin.

She moaned softly and the sound spurred him on. He felt her nipple harden, the pebble against his tongue, the other in his hand became taut while her groans increased. He couldn't stand the need for her any longer. Pulling his mouth away, he scooped her up, cradled her in his arms and carried her over to the bed.

Laying her down gently, he pulled her jeans off, leaving only her pink lace panties. His gaze drank her in. She was so beautiful. He pulled his own shirt off, then kicked off his shoes and pants. His erection stood at attention.

She leaned on her elbows looking at him and he remembered she had never been with a male before.

Most likely she had never seen one naked, either. He tempered his own needs and moved over to her. Taking her hand, he placed it on his chest. "You can touch everything you want to. Explore."

It was killing him, the blood throbbing in his organ to the point of exquisite pain, but he would suffer a lifetime in order to make sure she was comfortable. He stood still as she moved onto her knees, examining him, discovering every part of his maleness.

"Shift," She commanded, and the request surprised him.

"You mean…to a bear?"

"Yes. I want to see you in all of your forms."

He looked down at his erection. He'd never tried to shift in this state before, and he wasn't sure he could concentrate enough to do so. Yet, he was also concerned to not let her down. Closing his eyes, he focused on calling to his spirit guide in order to aid his change. At first nothing happened. Then he felt his fingernails elongate into claws. He was apperceptive to his fur coming through his pores. He fixated on shifting and soon he was standing before her, not as a man, but as a black bear on his hind quarters. She cautiously reached up and touched his fur. Her hand skimmed over his body.

He couldn't hold it. He tried to hold his form, but it was like trying to hold his breath. He couldn't last. Her touch sent a multitude of shivers into his very core. The blood gathered and made his dick harder, pulsating and throbbing with intense need. He morphed back into his human form, a sheen of sweat on his forehead from the exertion.

"Sorry. We're not really meant to change when we're so aroused. I'm a man first. My human needs will always prevail."

"I shouldn't have asked. I'm sorry. I was curious."

"It's okay, baby. Another time I'll show you anything you want, but right now. Right now, your touch, your look, fuck, your naked body is driving me through the roof with desire. I need you."

"I'm ready." Feather laid back onto the bed,

waiting.

He knew she was still unsure, still nervous, and he would do his best to make this easy for her. It still astounded him she had remained untouched for over 125 years. He leaned over her, tenderly kissing her. His hand caressed her skin, his shaft throbbing intensely. He wanted to be in her so desperately, he was sure he'd go insane. Yet, a part of him knew she was a virgin and he needed to go intensely slow before he could pluck her blossom from its bud.

Pushing up on his hands, his lips pressed against hers softly. With a gentleness, he moved down her body, spreading multiple kisses all over. She squirmed under him and made small gasps and moans.

After several long, agonizing minutes, he reached the top of her curly hair peeking out from the lace panties. He slid them off, his hands grazing every part of her smooth, silken legs. Moving slightly, he forced her legs apart, opening her up to him. Her aroused scent almost overwhelmed him and made his mouth water in anxiousness to taste her, to drink her juices. He admired her glistening sex before lowering his mouth to run his tongue over the edges of her outer lips.

He felt her almost jump, whether in surprise or shock he was unsure. He stopped and looked up at her. "You okay?" His voice was a low, husky growl, filled with desire.

"Yes. Don't stop. Please. Keep going." She should be horrified at being so exposed, but she wasn't. Ren soothed any anxieties she had and made her feel safe. He told her he was going to make love to her and maybe that was why she was so comfortable opening herself up to him. Then again, he made her body tingle so much, she didn't think she could resist even if she wanted to.

He smiled. "Oh, I have no intentions of stopping now, unless you tell me specifically to do so." He lowered his mouth back to her core, his tongue piercing the veil of her lips and dipping into the wetness already awaiting him. He groaned at her taste and lapped up her juices. He had to force himself to take long, slow, back-to-front-and-back-again licks. He planned on making this last as long as possible, until it became too much and he needed more. His tongue flicked her clit and she twisted her lower body. It was almost like she was trying to buck him off of her, but her hands had moved to his head, her bent knees rested tightly against his ears. She may turn her body from side to side, but she was not willing to let him go.

He knew her body was responding to him, even though she had no idea what was to come. He increased the intensity of his licking and suckling of her clit. When he was sure she was ready, he inserted first one finger, then two. He could feel her hymen, but that would come later. Instead, he focused on her g-spot and her clit. In moments, he had her bucking and calling his name as the power of her orgasm rose to break through the dam she had and spill over his fingers and tongue.

He lapped up every bit of her. When he was finished, he moved back up her body to rest on his elbows above her. His hand gently moved a strand of her hair off her face before he bent down to kiss her. Their tongues met once again in a dancing war. Feather had surrendered everything to him. Almost. A part of Ren was worried about taking her virginity, but he wanted to claim her for himself more than anything he could remember desiring.

When he lifted himself away from her mouth, she grinned. "I never tasted myself before. It's oddly erotic."

"You taste amazing, my wonderful cougar. But the real question is still in front of you. I won't proceed without your permission."

"You have it. I want it all. I want to feel everything, to know what I've been missing, and realize what I've avoided all this time. I think I've been waiting for you all my life, I just never realized it until now. I trust you. I…love you." There. She said it. It was the first time she told anyone who wasn't her brother she loved them. To her, those words were not frivolously said. They meant something. They were a depth of feeling rarer than anything in the universe, and the descriptions of love she'd read or heard about were finally realized by her because of Ren.

He seemed to know those words didn't come easy for her, that she wouldn't say them as an offhand comment or without a strong depth of meaning. He searched her eyes, her face, reconfirming the intensity of her words. His own eyes softened as he gazed into hers. "Thank you. I'll not betray those words, or you. I don't say those words lightly, either, and I'm not saying them now because I don't want to make you feel like I said them as a result of the situation. I'll say them when they will have greater meaning and you'll know the truth of them. I don't need the words to know how I feel about you, or how I've always felt about you, even when I didn't realize it. I can still stop, although it will be the hardest thing I'd ever do. Tell me to stop and I will."

"I know you would. I don't want you to stop. I'll wait for you to say those words to me when you're ready and I'll know them for the truth they are. Just as I hope you'll understand I didn't say them now because I am lying naked under you or because of that amazing world-shaking orgasmic release I just experienced. I said them because that's how I truly feel."

He chuckled and leaned down to kiss her lightly. "I know. I know. I'm very sorry. This is going to hurt a little, but it won't last long. I promise. Then, I'll blow your mind beyond world-shaking."

He moved so the tip of his shaft was against the opening of her sex. Slowly, he entered her slick core, allowing her to adjust to his size. When he came against her barrier, he stopped. He leaned down to kiss her deeply, pulling back just slightly to gain leverage to push through and break her cherry. He could feel her gasp, her hands clutching at his biceps when he did so. Within moments, Feather began to relax, the pain dissipating. Once he felt her relax, he slowly thrust his hips against her.

And his little cougar roared to life beneath him. She gripped him tightly, her nails raking his back. Her legs wrapped around his hips as she met his thrusts. She became alive for the first time in her life. She felt more connected with the universe than she ever had before. The feeling of him inside her, filling her up, was beyond her wildest imaginations or any of the stories she ever read. Nothing could describe what she was feeling. Her whole body tingled with intense sensations.

His thrusts increased in speed and she felt herself building again. Her muscles tightened, her breath hitched as she continued to moan. She felt like he was still growing inside her with each push into her body. His cock felt heavier against her womb, her walls felt as if they needed to get wider with each push. Then she felt his warmth jut out of his body into hers and it set her off once more. She exploded, her body stiffening as it quivered with yet another release. He thrust a couple more times, holding her as they both finished their spasms, then collapsed on top of her, rolling her to the side. He remained inside of her, not quite willing to let her go just yet.

He kissed her forehead, her cheeks, her nose, her lips. "Are you okay?" His concern was evident.

"I didn't know. I could never have guessed it could be like that. Is it always like that?"

He chuckled and kissed her lips again as he smiled. "No. It's only like that when you care about the person you're with. Otherwise, it's just exercise."

"Can we exercise with feeling some more?"

He laughed harder. "So, my little lion likes it. We can exercise like this as many times as you want, as long as I have a little time to recoup in between. I'm faster than a normal human male, but I will still need a couple of minutes to get the blood to flow back down there again."

Feather smiled. "I did okay?"

Ren became serious. "No, baby. You did great. All you ever have to do is be natural and you will always be great." He leaned over to brush his lips over hers. God damn but what she did to him.

Her grin widened as she could feel him getting hard inside of her again. It didn't take him long at all. He rolled onto his back, taking her with him, making sure he remained inside. His hands on her hips, he guided her into a rocking motion, showing how to ride him to her own satisfaction. He'd raised his hips to pump into her body once she established the rhythm of her ride. He focused on holding back, stilling her when he needed a moment to calm down. He was bound and determined to make her come a few more times before he would allow himself to release inside her again.

When the time came to explode inside of her, when he could hold off no longer, he used his hands and his hips to quicken her pace, bouncing her on his rod like a dancer in a strip club. She learned quickly, using her body's weight and her own rocking motion to build towards her release. The change in speed and his grunting sounds indicated to her that he was also getting close and, this time, he would topple over. The idea excited her, made her tighten even more against him. Moments later she cried out, exploding. Her raw sex dripping juices onto his pubic hair and mingling with his own hot seed as he spurted into her body.

She quivered, collapsing on top of him,

exhausted. Ren rubbed his hands on her back, catching his own breath as he listened to her. Although he was perfectly willing to stay like this forever, he knew they needed to clean up a bit. He had taken her virginity and there was a bit of residual effect from that. She would be sore and he easily stepped back into the role of wanting to care for her.

He gently rolled her over and removed himself from inside her body. She moaned once she was free of him, her eyes wide as he moved to get out of the bed. He scooped her up, carrying her into the bathroom, and sat her on the counter while he ran a bath for her to help clean her up. With extreme care, he lifted her and set her into the bath. Kneeling beside the tub, he washed her with a tender hand. "How do you feel?"

"Like a real woman," she replied softly, leaning over to kiss him.

He finished washing her, helping her stand before he joined her, turning on the shower to rinse off and washing himself in the process. After he dried her off, then himself, he carried her back to bed and curled up around her. He planned on never leaving her side again.

Epilogue

Ren held Feather's hand as they stood on the steps of the Bexar County Courthouse. He brought her hand up to his lips and kissed it before tucking it close against his chest.

"Are you sure you're okay? You don't have to be here for this."

"Yeah, I kinda do. It was me he kidnapped, and I've been called in to testify against him."

"I know, but still, if you don't want to be here, we'll figure something out. However, I'll be with you the whole time. You get nervous or anything, you just look at me, okay?"

Feather gave him a gentle smile before leaning over to kiss his cheek. "I know it's silly, but I'm cold."

Ren released her hand and wrapped his arm around her, rubbing her arm to stimulate blood flow. "It's just nerves. You've not seen him in months. He put you through a hell of a lot. It's going to be okay."

Feather rested her head on his shoulders as she looked around at the people who were arriving up the steps and entering the doors behind them. It was a few minutes later before she saw the couple. Lifting her head, she smiled and ran down the couple of steps to almost tackle the tall male of the pair.

"I've not seen you in days!" she exclaimed, pouting slightly.

"I know, Spud. Been busy unpacking in the new house. When Spitfire and I get it all fixed up, you and Ren will be our first dinner guests." He squeezed her in a tight hug, then let her go to shake hands with Ren while she moved to hug Apple.

Raine pulled Ren close in a bro hug while they shook hands. "She still looks happy, so you get to live another day."

Ren patted his back as he replied. "I see Shade hasn't shot you yet, so you must be doing good, too."

It was a running joke between the two men to make sure the women they originally protected were taken care of and loved continuously by the other.

As the women pulled apart, each of the men got on the other side of the ladies, respectively, and looked up at the imposing building. "I guess we should go in," Feather eventually stated, albeit she was dreading it. Raine even more so, since he had talked to Payne in prison shortly after he was incarcerated. Raine was left with too many concerns about Payne and what would happen the more time he spent in prison, in front of humans who didn't age quite the same way. Having him escape and be free to continue his mental delusions, murdering more innocents, including Apple and Feather, concerned him greatly.

They had to undergo an intense ritual to break the mental hold Payne had on Apple, and Raine sure as hell didn't want to go through anything like it ever again. Not that he wouldn't volunteer for anything to keep Apple safe, nor complete any ritual that tied him to her as this one had, but to share his past with her, for her to see all he had gone through as a child, concerned him.

The only way to have broken Payne's lock was to replace it with a stronger connection. Raine had volunteered. Apple and he had already talked about becoming mates, so it was the natural progression in preventing Payne from ever controlling her again. The Marble-seed and Breadroot would prevent Payne from attempting to hypnotize anyone in the future, such as the guards to open their doors and let him walk, but Raine still didn't want to consider having to do it again for anyone else. He would hate for Ren to have to consider something similar for Feather. They bore too many secrets, too much pain, too much abuse to want to let the person they loved ever see that part of them.

Ren held the door open for the other three and followed them inside the building and down the hall to the courtrooms. Feather stopped abruptly and it took a moment for Ren to understand why. Raine and Apple were both puzzled as Feather suddenly ran towards a tall, lanky male in a business suit. His hair pulled back into a ponytail, turquoise bolo tie replaced a cloth one. He was sharp looking, handsome, yet there was something primitive and virile about him. He quirked a smile as Feather leapt on him in a huge hug, his strong arms wrapping around her waist, lifting her off the ground for a moment before setting her back down.

"Austin. What on Earth are you doing here?" She was breathless as she stepped back. Ren stepped up and shook Austin's hand while Feather turned to Raine and Apple. "Guys, this is Austin. We trained at the camp centuries ago and he is currently Xulth's apprentice. Austin, this is my brother, Raine, and his mate, Shade. Ren, you might remember. He's the one who picked us up from the station when we first arrived."

Austin shook hands with each of them in turn. "Nice to meet you. Ren? It's been a long while."

"Yes. It has. What brings you here?"

"Payne River."

"What do you mean? What are you going to do?"

"I'm here to transfer him, per the court system,

into our custody."

"Our custody?" Ren asked, surprised. "Who is our?"

Raine balked with concern immediately. "Are you nuts? Do you even have a clue as to what he has done?"

Apple held onto Raine's arm, but even she was upset, her furrowed brow the only indication of being upset. Raine and Ren knew her well enough to know how affected she truly was. "It's not safe. Not for anyone if you set him free."

Austin held up his hands in surrender, asking for silence. "Our is Xulth and myself. We can deal with him. Dampen his powers, keep him at the mountain and away from everyone else. The humans can't be clued in to our longevity or powers. He is our concern, our burden and our brother. Therefore, we shall take on the responsibility."

"How are you going to get him? He won't go willingly. You understand the albatross you are going to be accountable for?" Raine wrapped his arm around Apple in order to control his temper at the possibility of Payne going free.

"We're aware, Raine. We're willing to accept what needs to be done. He will not harm anyone else ever again. You, your mate, your sibling, your friends will all be protected and humans will continue to remain in ignorance of shifters."

Ren stepped up, pulling Feather back to his side. "Exactly how are you going to get the judge to hand him over to you? Or were you just going to break him out of prison?"

"I have an order by the courts to have him released into my custody. It's all legal and won't raise any red flags." Austin turned to look at Feather, his gaze turning soft. "May I?" He held his hand out towards her stomach.

Feather looked between Ren and Raine and shrugged. "I guess so." She was puzzled as to why, but it wasn't a harmful request, so she agreed.

Austin placed his hand on her belly and smiled before removing it. The question was clearly written on Feather's face and he couldn't resist the fact she didn't know. The ring on her left ring finger glinted brightly, indicating she had found her mate and Ren seemed the perfect choice. "I'm happy for you and Ren," Austin said. "And for the new life you are going to be bringing in soon."

"New life?" Feather was floored, but not any more so than Ren, who looked like he was about to faint.

"I'm going to be an uncle?" Raine beamed proudly as he looked over at Feather. "Guess this means we need to work harder, Spitfire, in order to keep up."

Apple snorted derisively. "Speak for yourself. I told you before, I ain't giving up my job, and pregnancy sounds like that's the perfect way for that to happen. Now if you want to keep practicing, I'm all for that."

"Please. My ears are going to bleed if you two keep that up." Feather turned back to Austin. "You're sure?"

Austin nodded. "Was always my special gift. He is going to be a powerful one. We will be seeing him in about twelve years or so."

Worriedly, she looked over at Ren, but the smile on his face averted all fears she might have had. "You know, it might've been nice if I was able to find out normally and told him myself." Feather slugged Austin's shoulder, partly in jest.

"I told you now because you don't need to go into the courtroom. You don't need to see Payne ever again. You don't need that stress and neither does your son. I have everything under control."

"Son?" Ren couldn't have felt more ill or more proud than he did at that moment. He wanted to scream from the rooftops that he was going to be a dad.

Feather smiled. She was well aware he wanted a big family like his own, the start of which was now growing inside of her. "You're going to get your wish of a big family. Guess we're starting sooner than planned, though." She leaned over to Ren. "You're the only one I would want to be the father to my children. I know you'll be great at it."

Ren turned and kissed her. He was beyond

thrilled, beyond words. He was going to be a dad!

Raine moved over to Feather and lifted her slightly off her feet in a hug. "Congrats, Spud." Then he slugged Ren's arm. "Good to know you're shooting straight."

Feather turned back to Austin. "Don't you think it best I at least see him? I was the one he was obsessed with, after all."

"Which is precisely why you're better off letting him get you out of his mind."

Ren pulled Feather back. "He's right, you know. Letting Austin take Payne back to the mountain camp is the perfect solution. Payne will be under control, get the help and guidance he needs, and it will keep the humans from ever suspecting anything. Not seeing you at this point in time is a boon, a way for him to hopefully move on. You have more than just yourself to think about now, and I don't want any additional strain on you. You're carrying our young. That's more important to me."

Austin held his hand out to them, shaking one

Shifter's Pride

at a time. "It was good to meet you." When he finally got to Feather, he smiled. "It was great to see you again, Feather. Xulth sends his love." Austin turned, picked up a briefcase he had sitting on the floor by the wall and left the four of them standing outside the courtroom as he went in to present his case to the judge.

Raine shrugged. "I'm buying breakfast. We have to celebrate."

Moving his arm around Apple's neck, he swung her around and headed back towards the building's exit. Ren shrugged and did the same to Feather. "We are going to have to look at turning Raine's old room into a nursery."

Feather let Ren lead her away, only giving a momentary backwards glance to the closed courtroom doors. "We have time. We have lots of time."

ABOUT THE AUTHOR

She lives in the suburbs of Chicago with her three companions, all males... cats. She travels as much as she can to various Author/Reader conventions and loves to meet established fans and make new ones, some of which she considers friends more than fans.

More from Laura Hawks

Flaming Retribution

Laura Hawks

The Ghost and the Grimoire

Laura Hawks

DEMON'S KISS
LAURA HAWKS

DEMON'S DREAM
LAURA HAWKS

DEMON'S WEB

LAURA HAWKS

Made in the USA
San Bernardino, CA
07 May 2017